TEN THINGS

TEN THINGS YOUR ENEMY DOESN'T KNOW

TEN THINGS YOUR ENEMY DOESN'T KNOW THAT CAN HELP YOU:

If You Are a Christian

by

Dr. Horace L. Patterson, Sr.

Printed by R.H. Boyd Publishing Corporation
Nashville, Tennessee

**TEN THINGS YOUR ENEMY DOESN'T KNOW THAT CAN
HELP YOU: IF YOU ARE A CHRISTIAN**
Copyright © 2007 by R.H. Boyd Publishing Corporation

6717 Centennial Blvd.
Nashville, Tennessee 37209-1017

ISBN 1-58942-350-X

Patterson, Sr. Horace L.
Ten Things Your Enemy Doesn't Know that Can Help You: If You Are a Christian

TABLE OF CONTENTS

Chapter 10

Prayers

Introduction

There are ten things your enemies don't know that you need to know if you want to prevent their pleasure from becoming your pain. These ten bastions of knowledge can keep you warm when your enemies treat you cold and can make you strong when your enemies expect you to be weak. Rutherford D. Rogers said, "We're drowning in information and starving for knowledge." He was correct. The acquisition of information is not the equivalence of acquiring understanding. To know what something is is not the same thing as knowing what something means. To know that one is a father, mother, or leader is valuable information, but to know what it means to be a father, mother, or leader is to acquire understanding at a far more significant level. To gain the information that one is a child of God is a blessing, but to know what it means makes one more valuable to oneself and to the kingdom of God as a whole.

A small lad was selling puppies for $5. A man passed the boy's puppy station on the way to a business meeting in another city. The man's trip required a week's work prior to his return home. Knowing that he could not care for a small puppy during his week's sojourn, he resolved to purchase one after the completion of his assignment away from home. Upon his return, he was startled to see that the price of the puppies had risen from $5 to $25. When the man inquired of the lad why the cost had risen so quickly, the boy said, "Last week, their eyes were closed—now that their eyes are open, I think they are worth more." The buyer chuckled, bought the $25 puppy, and went his way. Whether the puppy's worth increased as a result of having its eyes open is debatable, but members of the kingdom of God always increase in value when their eyes are open to the myriad of enemies that Christians must face.

When the prophet Hosea said, "My people are destroyed for lack of knowledge" (Hos. 4:6, KJV), he was speaking of people who defined themselves as God's chosen people. These people did not simply view themselves as people created by God; they considered themselves to be people of God. However, according to the assessment of the prophet Hosea, they were being destroyed—not simply hurt, wounded, inconvenienced, or disturbed but destroyed—by a lack of knowledge.

What you don't know can enslave you. Thursday, January 1, 1863, was a crisp and bright day in Washington, D.C. President Abraham Lincoln signed the Emancipation Proclamation. The final draft read that slaves in designated territories "are, and henceforward shall be free." The great historian John Hope Franklin informs us that it was not until June 19, 1865, when Major General Gordon Granger landed at Galveston, Texas with the news that the war had ended, that the enslaved in Texas claimed their freedom. It was two and a half years after President Lincoln's proclamation that the impact of freedom was realized by those who had been set free. Two and a half years longer the bitter taste of slavery endured because the enslaved did not know that they had been set free.

Satan is real. Flesh and blood always are weak and sometimes quite wicked. You will have enemies because you are a child of God. While traversing the dry Palestinian soil of His day, Jesus found Himself in the midst of the tempest of a ferocious controversy. The battle was hot and, caught in the throes of tremendous assaults from the enemy, our Lord said to one group, "Ye are of your father the devil, and the lusts of your father ye will do. He was a murderer from the beginning, and abode not in the truth, because there is no truth in him. When he speaketh a lie, he speaketh of his own: for he is a liar, and the father of it" (John 8:44, KJV). Jesus spoke these words not to a spirit or to some spirits but to a group of

6

unconverted people. The people to whom our Lord spoke mistakenly thought they were children of Abraham, saying, "Abraham is our father" (John 8:39), but Jesus knew better. Jesus said, "Ye are of your father the devil" (v. 44).

The devil's children are everywhere. Satan has spawned his evil seed among all nations, all colors, all races, all lands, and all ages up to that time in the future where the apostle John says in Revelation 20:10, "And the devil that deceived them was cast into the lake of fire and brimstone, where the beast and the false prophet are, and shall be tormented day and night for ever and ever" (KJV). I have heard some well-meaning but foolishly misinformed and misguided people eulogize some Christians, saying "He/She never had one enemy." If he/she was a fruitful child of God, you can bank on the fact that the soul had a host of enemies because the devil's children are murderers just like their father. They are liars just like their father. They might look good, smell nice, speak impressively, and walk gracefully, but they are their father's children, and they will obey him even if they don't want to. God is the only almighty Being in the universe. God believes in free will. You can be His child and disobey Him. You can't be a child of the devil and disobey him because he is too insecure to allow you to exercise free will. God loves. Satan controls. Satan is like the insecure parent or mate that won't allow the object of his control to spend the night in a better home than his because he is afraid that he will lose what he has. God's gifts and provisions are so great that He allows free and open range travel because He knows that there is nothing better than what He has already given and what He has to offer. Every prodigal son and daughter eventually discovers this fact and returns home. The devil's children will attack God's children because they have to obey their controlling, ruling, and regulating, evil father. It has been said, "If you have something that you believe is yours, set it free. If it returns, it is yours forever—if it doesn't return, it never was yours in the first place." If you are a child of God, you will be attacked because you are God's goods. You are God's child and should always remember that, as God's child, you are never, ever an unprotected child. It takes courage, trust, and obedience to prevail. The devil is not all powerful or all knowing and neither are his children. There are some things that your enemies don't know that can give you the victory, regardless of the bleakness of the hour, the heat of the day, or the thickness of the night. For some situations, anger is okay, but never become an angry person. "He that is slow to anger is better than the mighty; and he that ruleth his spirit than he that taketh a city" (Prov. 16:32, KJV).

One of the sources of reward for your enemies is your ongoing, excessively expressed anger. "Don't let them see you sweat" is wisdom that you need to make into your personal property from time to time. Your enemies want to hear and see domineering expressions of your anger because most people know that anger is a mechanism of defense. If all you have is your anger and its tools in your hours of need, you don't have enough. If all you have to defend yourself is your anger, you don't have enough help to win the war. If all you can summon to save yourself when you are attacked is your anger, you will have some very happy enemies. "Make no friendship with an angry man; and with a furious man thou shalt not go: Lest thou learn his ways, and get a snare to thy soul" (Prov. 22:24-25, KJV). It is very important for you to remember that you attract what you are and not always what you want. In other words, you become similar to those with whom you spend a good deal of time. Two dead people simply make a larger funeral. Two angry people only double the frustration that comes from one angry person. Sometimes, you need to go to your address book and discard some phone numbers.

Justified anger is not identical to being an angry person. "Be ye angry, and sin not: let not the sun go down upon your wrath" (Eph. 4:26, KJV). Vented without discipline, anger can hurt the angry and destroy relationships that can be healed. Whatever you nurse and offer nourishment has a chance to live and grow. If you feed your lower self, it will become stronger than your higher self and rule your life in ways that will evict peace of mind from your earthly tent. If you cannot be at peace, you can never be at your best. The element of time is one factor that distinguishes the difference between being angry and being an angry person. How long you allow an act, person, or circumstance to unsettle and agitate you is a defining factor. Bottled anger makes for bitterness. Nourished anger leads to multiplication, and denied anger generates hypocrisy. Aristotle said, "It is easy to fly into a passion—anybody can do that, but to be angry with the right person to the right extent and at the right time and with the right object and in the right way—that is not easy, and it is not everyone who can do it." Not everyone can do it, but children of God who know the ten things that their enemies don't know can use anger in a healthy manner without becoming an angry person. Anger, in automotive terms, is okay to use as a brake pedal to make some necessary stops, but it is dangerous if we employ it as an accelerator to move us from where we are to where we ought to be. Your source for movement needs to pull you rather than drive you. Being pulled creates far less wear and tear on your life than being driven.

There is a wonderful piece of advice that says, "Never ask a barber if he thinks you need a haircut." The wisdom of that statement points out the sheer foolishness of asking those who are causing your problems to effectively instruct you on how to fix them. The plain truth is that the people who benefit from keeping your life in a state of discord will rarely work against their perceived self-interest. Apart from God's grace, neither you nor I are okay. Without the knowledge reserved for the children of the Kingdom, you will help your enemies hurt you and those you love. Those who are human-ists may be well meaning, but they have no working answers for people who are called to live victoriously by faith. The ten things your enemies don't know do not have to be ten things you can't plant your feet on. You can stand where others fall. You can win where others lose, and you can soar where others sink. Henry David Thoreau said, "I saw a delicate flower had grown up two feet high between the horses' feet and the wheel track...an inch more to the right or left had sealed its fate, or an inch higher. Yet it lived to flourish as much as if it had a thousand acres of untrodden space around it and never knew the danger it incurred. It did not borrow trouble, nor invite an evil fate by apprehending it." Knowledge enables you to bloom wherever you are planted. With the dream of yesterday, the vision of tomorrow, and the spiritual efforts of each and every God-given day, you can flourish even in small places as much as if you have "a thousand acres of untrodden space" around you. You only live this life once, but if you get it right, once is enough. If you are going to climb, you need to hold on to branches and not to blossoms. *Ten things Your Enemy Doesn't Know* will create branches for you to hold, and if you hold on to that which can hold you, you will be held up even when "the heathen rage, and the people imagine a vain thing" (Ps. 2:1, KJV).

If your enemies knew these ten things, they would no longer be your enemies. Let's hope, for their sake, they read this book. However, regardless of whether they do or not, you can water your own seeds, announce your own victory, and claim your own revelation because of the God to whom you belong.

CHAPTER I

Your Enemies Don't Know that Their Words and Deeds Against You Remove a Nasty Woe and Open Up a Better Door

Woe unto you, when all men shall speak well of you! for so did their fathers to the false prophets (Luke 6:26, KJV).

These are the words of Jesus. Jesus was not the kind of man who spent His life crying "Woe." Whenever Jesus used this term, He was deeply concerned about impending, salient, and serious sorrows. The same verse of Scripture from St. Luke, spoken by our Lord, could be rendered, "You have great sorrows when all people praise you! The ones who praise you had ancestors who also praised false prophets." The need for human applause and approval is deeply embedded in the human psyche, it encourages and molds us. It makes a baby take steps and learn to walk. It sends athletes to weight rooms and motivates hours, days, and years of practice for musicians. The notion of being well thought of drives human behavior to rise above basic instincts that might solicit disapproval and punishment from the herd.

A small girl, afraid of the dark, asked her mother to stay in her room until she went to sleep one night. The mother sought to comfort her by saying, "God will be with you." The child responded by saying, "I know that God will be with me, but I want somebody with some skin on them to be with me." This need of flesh to have flesh validate and accompany us can trip us up and send us out looking for vacancies in the front of parades in order to win the favor of the crowd. Instead of making a significant difference, we can become so

11

tame, groggy, and devitalized that we will be happy simply to make a salary regardless of what we have to do. As a Christian, you are not a participant in a parade, looking to win an award for the best float. You are a soldier in the army of the almighty God, striving to hear Him say, "Well done" rather than, "Well said." It takes balanced and sober living to strike the right medium between money and pleasing God.

Jesus says you have stepped across the line when "all men speak well of you." When people who ought to be your enemies aren't, something is wrong. When people who hate right and righteousness speak of you kindly, you have started walking in the wrong direction! If those to whom Satan points to with pride begin to point to you with glee, "woe unto you" is the message that is screaming for your attention. When unconverted, mean-spirited people who never sow with love or reap with thanksgiving attack you, they are affirming your worth to the Kingdom. When weak-willed crowd pleasers speak ill of you and when they rejoice when wrong is committed against you, pity them—even thank them—for you need not concern yourself about the verse, "Woe to you when all men speak well of you" (Luke 6:26, NIV). Jesus says, "Blessed are ye, when men shall hate you, and when they shall separate you from their company, and shall reproach you, and cast out your name as evil, for the Son of man's sake" (Luke 6:22, KJV). "Blessed are they which are persecuted for righteousness' sake: for theirs is the kingdom of heaven. Blessed are ye, when men shall revile you, and persecute you, and shall say all manner of evil against you falsely, for my sake. Rejoice, and be exceeding glad: for great is your reward in heaven: for so persecuted they the prophets which were before you" (Matt. 5:10-12, KJV).

A Badge of Honor

Learn to wear the attacks of your enemies as a badge of honor. Remember, you are on your feet in a heavyweight boxing match. The only time boxers stop swinging at the opposition is during rest periods or when one is knocked out and is on the mat. Child of God, your enemies can't knock you out because God won't let them. Stay on your feet and expect the opposition to throw some punches. You already know who is going to win the fight. Your enemies don't know that it is not your friends but their own persecution and perpetual evil that opens up the door to better blessings both in time and eternity. In the kingdom of God, Jesus establishes this unique formula—persecution equals a great reward in heaven. He did not say *for* heaven but *in* heaven. If it is in heaven, you can draw off the interest in the here and the now.

Jesus taught His followers to lay up treasures in heaven, where thieves cannot steal and moths cannot corrupt (Matt. 6:20). While your enemies become worse off for what they do and say to harm you, their deeds do you a great service. They endorse your fruitfulness. They sanction your service. They bolster your standing in the community of goodness. They validate your usefulness. Your enemies don't know it, but they are endorsing your candidacy for a future promotion in a way that friendly references can never, ever accommodate. No sensible American wants to receive an award from Osama bin Laden. No wise African American wants to be given some plaque from the KKK, and no Christian worth his/her salt wants to be on good terms with the enemies of God. I am not speaking here of those tendencies that define a paranoid personality disorder. I also do not endorse a pattern of pervasive distrust and suspiciousness of others. (I don't want you to develop a cynical spirit that sends you out into the world always assuming that others are there to exploit, harm, or deceive you, even when there is no evidence to support that expectation.) God forbid that you move forth in your daily living suspecting, on the basis of little or no evidence, that others are plotting against you and may attack you at any time and without reason. I do not want you to become preoccupied with unjustifiable doubts about others that send you on some useless journey, minutely scrutinizing those around you for evidence of hostile intentions. People with paranoid personality disorders bear grudges and often are unwilling to forgive injuries or even insults that they think they have received. These people help their enemies because even minor slights arouse major hostility in their hearts, and they are consistently vigilant to the harmful intentions of others. This disorder creates pathological jealousy and often moves jealous-hearted people to gather trivial and circumstantial information to support their jealous beliefs and/or preconceived insults. People with these features are generally difficult to get along with and have severe problems with close relationships. Their excessive suspiciousness and hostility may be seen in argumentativeness, recurrent complaining, or hostile and quiet aloofness. The remarkable reality of combative behavior and ongoing suspiciousness in their nature often elicits hostile responses in others, which then serve to confirm their original expectations.

With all that said, a good friend of mine who worked for me when I was the director of Chronic Care in Community Mental Health once said, "Just because you believe that people are after you don't mean that they aren't." He was right. Christians never should allow paranoid attitudes to dominate their outlooks, but they should remember that we follow a Savior who bore a cross. He set out with high dreams and holy purposes. Neither the dreams nor the purposes were blighted out by the grim and gruesome cross, but the failure of the cross should never cause us to forget the reality of the cross. "And there followed him a great company of people, and of women, which also bewailed and lamented him. But Jesus turning unto them said, Daughters of Jerusalem, weep not for me, but weep for yourselves, and for your children. For, behold, the days are coming, in the which they shall say, Blessed are the barren, and the wombs that never bare, and the paps which never gave suck. Then shall they begin to say to the mountains, Fall on us; and to the hills, Cover us. For if they do these things in a green tree, what shall be done in the dry?" (Luke 23:27-31, KJV). Like the enemies of our Lord, some of our enemies will find it easy to insult us as we threaten to fall under the weight of a cross that seems too heavy to bear. Bear their scorn because you know something that they don't know. You never miss the best when you follow the Lord of love and life. The words and deeds of your enemies must not be permitted by you to cause you to be ungrateful for their eternal meaning. What is their measure of meaning? They mean you have another star in your crown, another present under your tree, another testimony for your story, another blessing for your praise, and another opportunity for you to practice shining on this earth before you begin to shine forever in eternity.

Don't let the words "I hate you" from enemies deafen you to the message "I am using you" from God

> And Jehoshaphat said, Is there not here a prophet of the LORD besides, that we might inquire of him? And the king of Israel said unto Jehoshaphat, There is yet one man, Micaiah the son of Imlah, by whom we may inquire of the LORD: but I hate him; for he doth not prophesy good concerning me, but evil. And Jehoshaphat said, Let not the king say so (1 Kings 22:7-8, KJV).

The desire to live in a fool's paradise of flattering self delusions often moves people to hate the truths that the people of God stand for. Don't allow yourself to worry when men express their hatred. God's laws and purposes are accomplished through the vessels that He uses, regardless of human and demonic hate. The king who said, "I hate him" also said, "He is a prophet of the living God." The king's own words defined the prophet Micaiah as a faithful and effective messenger of the God who cannot lie. The king said, "I hate him"; the facts said, "God is using him." Ahab, due to King Jehoshaphat's insistence, sent for Micaiah. Ahab called Micaiah his enemy, but he had to send for him in order to receive a true word of prophecy from the Lord. It's interesting that even though the king despised Micaiah, he went looking for him. Micaiah did not have to maneuver himself to such a position, but his God-given gift made room for him. When God is using you, He makes you impossible to ignore. "Ah Lord God! Behold, thou hast made the heaven and the earth by thy great power and stretched out arm, and there is nothing too hard for thee: Thou shewest lovingkindness unto thousands, and recompenses the iniquity of the fathers into the bosom of their children after them: the Great, the Mighty God, the LORD of hosts, is his name. Great in counsel, and mighty in work: for thine eyes are open upon all the ways of the sons of men: to give every one according to his ways, and according to the fruit of his doings" (Jer. 32:17-19, KJV). The God who is great in counsel and mighty in work labors to make His instruments impassable. God's truth is like a seed that lives in our bodies, and the buds and fragrances of it blossom in our hearts, regardless of what people or systems do or fail to get done.

Sent for because God made them impassable

Sometimes, God ordains and anoints you as a force to be reckoned with. It's not that people want to deal with you—it's just a fact that they can't get around dealing with you. Sometimes, God decrees that the bus can't leave without you being seated and the job can't be done right unless you are involved in the process. Glue yourself to the promises of God, and He will fulfill them. You might be promoted by God to be over some things, and you should be thankful but remember the example of Joseph.

16

1. Pharaoh sent for Joseph. "Then Pharaoh sent and called Joseph, and they brought him hastily out of the dungeon: and he shaved himself, and changed his raiment, and came in unto Pharaoh. And Pharaoh said unto Joseph, I have dreamed a dream, and there is none that can interpret it: and I have heard say of thee, that thou canst understand a dream to interpret it. And Joseph answered Pharaoh, saying, It is not in me: God shall give Pharaoh an answer of peace" (Gen. 41:14-16, KJV). Joseph was placed over Egypt when he was in Egypt, but he was never of Egypt. When he died, he was so glued to God's promise of another home that he required his family to take his bones to that land when God led them out of Egypt.

2. Jesse sent for David. "Again, Jesse made seven of his sons to pass before Samuel. And Samuel said unto Jesse, The Lord hath not chosen these. And Samuel said unto Jesse, Are here all thy children? And he said, There remaineth yet the youngest, and, behold, he keepeth the sheep. And Samuel said unto Jesse, Send and fetch him: for we will not sit down till he come hither. And he sent, and brought him in. Now he was ruddy, and withal of a beautiful countenance, and goodly to look to. And the Lord said, Arise, anoint him: for this is he. Then Samuel took the horn of oil, and anointed him in the midst of his brethren: and the spirit of the Lord came upon David from that day forward. So Samuel rose up, and went to Ramah" (1 Sam. 16:10-13, KJV).

3. Zedekiah sent for Jeremiah. "When Jeremiah was entered into the dungeon, and into the cabins, and Jeremiah had remained there many days; Then Zedekiah the king sent, and took him out: and the King asked him secretly in his house, and said, Is there any word from the Lord? And Jeremiah said, There is: for, said he, thou shalt be delivered into the hand of the King of Babylon. Moreover Jeremiah said unto King Zedekiah, What have I offended against thee, or against they servants, or against this people, that ye have put me in prison? Where are now your prophets which prophesied unto you, saying, The King of Babylon shall not come against you, nor against this land?" (Jer. 37:16-19, KJV).

4. Ahab sent for Micaiah. While waiting, the 400 false prophets told King Jehoshaphat and Ahab that victory was assured if they attacked the King of Syria in order to reclaim the lost property of Ramoth in Gilead. Zedekiah, a leader of the 400 false prophets, made iron horns to reveal how Israel would prevail in battle. The false prophets shouted out their approval. They were excited, but it takes much more than excitement to be successful in this world or any other when God's favor does not rest upon your goals. Upon his arrival, Micaiah lied to Ahab. He told him to proceed with his plans. Ahab knew that the prophet was not speaking the truth and said so. The forthcoming truth announced God's judgment, which included Israel's defeat and Ahab's death. Micaiah's parting words to Ahab were, "If you ever return safely, the Lord has not spoken through me" (1 Kings 22:28, NIV). Ahab died as the prophet said he would. Ahab's death fulfilled the prophecy, thus revealing the difference between the real and the counterfeit and the godly and the ungodly. It was both the deeds and the death of Ahab that spoke a clear word about how our enemies remove that nasty "woe unto you when all men speak well of you." His death and deeds are also reminders of how God uses us to accomplish His desires in the midst of enemy hatred. If Ahab had known that his deeds and his death would forever stand as a testimony that God had spoken to Micaiah, he probably would have postponed the war and kept his opinions of the prophet to himself. Your enemies speak ill of you because they don't know that the very words they speak will eventually buoy your vessel as you sail beyond their expectations, regardless of whether those forecasts are formed in elegance or spewed in raw hostility.

CHAPTER II

Your Enemies Don't Know that God Has a Bag for Your Sins and a Book and a Bottle for Your Tears

> My transgression is sealed up in a bag, and thou sewest up mine iniquity (Job 14:17, KJV). Thou tellest my wanderings: put thou my tears into thy bottle: are they not in thy book? (Ps. 56:8, KJV)

God has a book for your tears. Your enemies have a book for your sins. God bottles your tears. Your enemies bask in your troubles. When Job employed the figure of sin being bagged up, he drew upon what was an effective custom during his day. Oriental merchants and monarchs carefully deposited certain sums of money and gold into securely sewn bags. The bag would be sealed until it reached the proper destination. No carrier or courier could break the seal. The seal remained intact from hand to hand, and the exact sum contained was untouched until it reached the proper source empowered to break the seal and examine its contents. Legal records were also kept in bags that were sealed until the need presented itself to have the records produced and scrutinized. The bag might have traveled great distances across barren plains and rugged terrain, during all kinds of weather. Eventually, the bag was opened but only by the proper authority.

Your enemy might be your supervisor at work or your leader in some enterprise. Your enemy might be a co-worker, acquaintance, a member of your blood family, or someone you barely know or don't know at all. Your enemy could be someone whose self-esteem is threatened simply because of the way you govern your life, handle adversity, or wear success or sorrow. Your enemy could be the source that gets close enough to you to make sure that you experience a coldness that has an unusual quality that is distinctively personal and deceptively chilling. Your enemy could be the unrecognized root cause that works day and night to keep you from receiving affirmation and appreciation: "Faithful are the wounds of a friend; but the kisses of an enemy are deceitful" (Prov. 27:6, KJV). Snakes kill with their mouths, and they strike at objects in motion. You might not feel like you are making any progress, doing any good, or advancing toward worthy goals, but your enemies' assaults upon you are based upon your motion as perceived by them and not your actual success. In other words, your enemies may experience your successes far more poignantly than you do. In simple terms, your enemies see you doing far more than you see yourself doing. There are many who wish that they could be where you are, doing as well as you are. Their actions and reactions to harm you are often indicators that the light is on and is shining in the darkness. Snakes are as blind as bats. They can't see, but their tongues are more sensitive to motion than any movement detector escalating from the mind of humankind. So, just remember that when your enemy strikes at you, you must be moving.

"And this is the condemnation, that light is come into the world, and men loved darkness rather that light, because their deeds were evil. For every one that doeth evil hateth the light, neither cometh to the light, lest his deeds should be reproved" (John 3:19-20, KJV). No matter how much your enemies resent it, your sins are in a bag that is thick enough to hide them because the blood of Jesus is impenetrable. Your works shine because God is shining through you, even when you can't see results or when you don't feel like anything is shimmering. Acts 5:15 provides us with a marked and dramatic illustration of how God uses us to accomplish feats beyond our anticipation and knowledge. "Insomuch that they brought forth the sick into the streets, and laid them on beds and couches, that at the least the shadow of Peter pass-ing by might overshadow some of them" (KJV). The Bible does not say that the sick people were healed, but from the way in which the Holy Spirit records this event, it is no stretch to assume that the sick were healed. If no healings took place, you can be certain that the sick would not have been carried into the streets for very long, and you can, with equal certainty, rest assured that no indignation would have escalated from our Lord's enemies. "There came also a mul-titude out of the cities round about unto Jerusalem, bringing sick folks, and them which were vexed with unclean spirits: and they were healed every one. Then the high priest rose up, and all they that were with him, (which is the sect of the Sadducees,) and were filled with indignation" (Acts 5:16-17, KJV).

By using Peter's shadow, God was using an intangible product that rested behind the back of Peter. Peter's first mir-acle of shadow healing was probably something he didn't even know about. Somebody had to tell him about it even though God was using him to do it. As long as God used the shadow of Peter to heal, someone else saw the healing before Peter heard about it. As Peter walked forward, God blessed people by using the shadow that was behind him. You never know all the good God is doing through you, but your ene-mies will always see enough miracles to cause them to burn with indignation. This is an ongoing source of intense frus-tration to them because they have written your sins down in their books, but the only things shining through you are those bright lights that exasperate their dark world. You are a mystery to them. They know that you are a sinner, but your sins don't dominate, define, or subjugate you. They know that you are not perfect, but your imperfections don't bend you to their wills, and they don't know why. "It's just not nat-ural," they complain to their lower selves, and they are right. It's not natural; it's supernatural! We all know what David did with Bathsheba. It's enough to destroy a legacy, but it didn't. Somehow, David's faults were swallowed up in the greater glory of being "a man after God's own heart." Abraham's faith failed him in Egypt, but somehow, the imperious verdict of history is, "He was the Father of the faithful." We know that Hadassah had been occupying the role of Esther for so long that she responded to the urgent call of Mordecai with a statement about protocol. However, the phrase that rules the roost in defining her is not what she said about protocol but when she said, "I am going to see the king. If I perish, I perish." So, your enemies ask why life, time, and history don't view you through the prism of their personal perspective. It is this ongoing frustration that dominates their view of you. They see you as a threat to their peace of mind and their ability to interpret the world in a way that gives them some sense of control. In your eyes, your enemies might appear to out-distance you in many ways, but through the corridors of their egotistical mindset, your very presence threatens their well-being.

The arrival of the Christ Child created a meeting place for both adoration and assassination in ancient Bethlehem. The wise men came to adore Him. Herod's solders marched double-time to assassinate Him. This strange but real discrepancy in assessment led to the wise men saying, "Where is he that is born King of the Jews? for we have seen his star in the east, and are come to worship him" (Matt. 2:2, KJV). The same birth that moved angels to praise God in the visible heavens and saturate the night air with Christmas lyrics ringing from their lips also resulted in the declaration, "Then Herod, when he saw that he was mocked of the wise men, was exceeding wroth, and sent forth, and slew all the children that were in Bethlehem, and in all the coasts thereof, from two years old and under, according to the time which he had diligently inquired of the wise men. Then was fulfilled that which was spoken by Jeremy the prophet, saying,

In Rama was there a voice heard, lamentation, and weeping, and great mourning, Rachel weeping for her children, and would not be comforted, because they are not" (Matt. 2:16-18, KJV).

The arrival of the Christ Child triggered the paranoid behavior of an insecure, wretched, wicked, and determined enemy of God. Your arrival and departure is in God's hands, and you trigger things in the invisible realm. Your earthly enemies' assessment of your sins nags them into states of restlessness and even sleeplessness because they cannot determine the boundaries of your comings or goings. They see that you receive better treatment than you deserve. What or whom God keeps is well kept. What or whom God does not keep is as a seed moving at the mercy of any vagrant wind. By the way, your enemies are right. You and I do receive better treatment from God than we deserve.

"Except the Lord build the house, they labor in vain that build it: except the Lord keep the city, the watchman waketh but in vain. It is vain for you to rise up early, to sit up late, to eat the bread of sorrows: for so he giveth his beloved sleep" (Ps. 127:1-2, KJV). The transgressor often can't sleep, in spite of sleep aids and long hours of creating one mess after another. David says of the transgressor, "He deviseth mischief upon his bed; he setteth himself in a way that is not good; he abhorreth not evil" (Ps. 36:4, KJV). David contrasts this turbulent state of wicked existence by saying of the godly, "They shall be abundantly satisfied with the fatness of thy house; and thou shalt make them drink of the river of thy pleasures. For with thee is the fountain of life: in thy light shall we see light." (Ps. 36:8-9, KJV). Think with me on this assertion that David makes when he says, "Thou shalt make them drink of the river of thy pleasures." This teaches us a great lesson about God's determination to bless His children. He won't just lead us, guide us, or direct our steps; He will make us drink of the river of His pleasures. God created the

23

law of gravity and put it on display in an apple tree. God then gave Sir Isaac Newton the brains and the pleasurable pursuit of knowledge as He watched an apple fall from the apple tree. God created shoe polish from a peanut and gave Dr. George Washington Carver the pleasure of discovery as he drank from the river of knowledge. God created honey and divided it up. He put part of it in the honeybee and the other part into a flower. God then gave the honeybee a natural love for flower petals. Therefore, when the honeybee makes honey, it is not only doing something it ought to do; it is doing something it loves to do. God makes His people drink from the river of His pleasures. When I bless someone, I am not only doing what I ought to do; I am doing what I love to do. Feeding the hungry, clothing the naked, sharing the Gospel, reclaiming a lost sheep, winning a lost soul, and lifting the lonely are not just things I have to do; they are things that I love to do. Your enemies can't figure it out, but they sense that you've got something they missed, and sometimes, it keeps them up at night, and "they devise mischief on their beds."

1. They Don't Know Where the Bag Is. There are, at least, two repugnant reasons for your enemies' wretchedness concerning your bagged sins. The first is due to the fact that they can't open the bag that God has sewn up. The second is, they don't know where the bag is. The prophet Isaiah speaks with a voice within his voice to the ear within our ear, revealing the location of the bag. "Behold, for peace I had great bitterness: but thou hast in love to my soul delivered it from the pit of corruption: for thou hast cast all my sins behind thy back" (Isa. 38:17, KJV). At Calvary, God the Father turned His back on Jesus. "Eloi, Eloi, lama sabachthani" translated into English means "My God, my God, why hast thou forsaken me?" (Matt. 27:46, KJV). God has counted our sins, dropped them behind His back, and planted them into the pit of oblivion. The grave of Jesus and the cry of forsakenness from the cross are located behind the back of God. The back of God is unreachable because, in the language of our forebears, "He is too wide to go around, even as He is too high to go over and too deep to go under" (see Eph. 3:16-19; Isa. 55:8-9). The word "forsaken" in Greek is the word *egkataleipo.* It means "to leave in the lurch." The word "lurch" can be defined as "a losing position" or "a very difficult place." Now, the question of our Lord means, "God how can You leave me at this time, in this state, without an answer and without a solution?" This is the only place in the Bible where Jesus asked the Father, "Why?". Jesus faced His antagonist in the wilderness, where nights were cold and shadows were long, for 40 days and nights, and He never asked, "Why?". Our Lord was not an insecure entrepreneur who needed public endorsements from a famous figure. Therefore, when Judas betrayed and Peter denied, He never asked, "Why?". It was only when the bag of our sins was removed from behind the back of the Father and planted on Him that He asked, "Why?". It was only then, when the intimate eternal relationship that an only begotten Son could have with His Father was broken, that our Lord cried, "Why?". In His cry, He addressed God as God. Jesus prayed for His enemies, saying, "Father, forgive them; for they know not what they do" (Luke 23:34, KJV). Jesus prayed a prayer of victory, saying, "Father, into thy hands I commend my spirit" (Luke 23:46, KJV). How amazing it is that Jesus addressed the Father as "Father" on each occasion that He spoke to Him from the cross except the moment in which our bag of sins was thrown from behind the Father's back onto His sinless shoulders. Paul helps us at this point to grasp as much of the divine transaction as the human mind is capable of understanding "For he hath made him to be sin for us, who knew no sin; that we might be made the righteousness of God in him" (2 Cor. 5:21, KJV).

So dark, so evil, so corrupt, so vile, so heinous, and so foul was the scene that the Father, in His holiness, was compelled to turn His back upon Jesus as if He did not exist. He, who was no sinner, became sin and descended into the very depths, where Satan danced, in order to break the power of sin and make believers righteous with the certified righteousness of God through Him. No devil, demon, or person can undo what has been done. God, the Father, turned His back on God, the Son, so He would never have to turn His back on you. At Calvary, behind the back of God, Jesus paid it all. At Calvary, behind the back of God, Jesus faced the consequences of sin and buried them in His perfect sacrifice. Your enemies can't condemn you because "There is therefore now no condemnation to them which are in Christ Jesus, who walk not after the flesh, but after the Spirit" (Rom. 8:1, KJV). Your enemies are right when they say you get treated better than you deserve because "He hath not dealt with us after our sins; nor rewarded us according to our iniquities. As far as the east is from the west, so far hath he removed our transgressions from us" (Ps. 103:10, 12, KJV).

Your enemies are frustrated because their book is defeated by God's bag. He says, "I, even I, am he that blotteth out thy transgressions for mine own sake, and will not remember thy sins" (Isa. 43:25, KJV). Your enemies are multiplying your sins daily, but they don't know that God has already resolved them through subtraction. Child of the King, if you are ever tempted to buy into your enemies' assessments, heed this mighty word that says, "Let us draw near with a true heart in full assurance of faith, having our hearts sprinkled from an evil conscience, and our bodies washed with pure water" (Heb. 10:22, KJV). Where is the bag for your sins? What is the bag for your sins? It is the sacred, broken, bruised, crimeless, holy, and bloodless body of Jesus. There is no blood left in the body of Jesus. He shed it all on the cross. When the blood of Jesus was released, it was totally released. It took all of His blood to get the job done that the holiness of God intended and purposed.

In the eyes of your enemies, you are far from what you ought to be in order to be treated as well as you are. But praises be to God that, in the sight that really counts, you are just what you need to be on a scale of one to ten. Because of the bag you are a perfect dozen, and that means, in the language of my teenage daughter, Ivy, "You're off the hook."

2. Counted as Righteous. In the fourth chapter of Romans, Paul says, "Abraham believed God, and it was counted unto him for righteousness" (v. 3, KJV). The Hebrew word for "believe," once translated, means "to say Amen." God gave a promise, and Abraham responded with "Amen," which means, "so be it." It was that kind of faith that was counted by God for righteousness, and it still is. God put your sins on Christ's account so that He could put Christ's righteousness on your account. The sixteenth chapter of Leviticus describes the Jewish Day of Atonement. The high priest at the altar was presented with two goats. One was chosen to be slain as a sacrifice. Its blood was taken into the Holy of Holies and sprinkled on the Mercy Seat. The Mercy Seat was the golden cover on the Ark of the Covenant. That shed blood temporarily met the righteous demands of the holy God. The high priest then put his hands on the head of the second goat, confessed the sins of the people, and then sent it away into the wilderness. The blood of animals could never take away sin, but it could cover sin for a while. Behind the back of God, Jesus purchased a finished salvation of righteousness for the believer. No thundercloud of judgment is on your trail. No eternal avenger hangs over your head. You might have to be corrected by God from time to time, but you never can be condemned by anyone because "The blood of Jesus will never lose its power." Sometimes, you can see tortured looks on the faces of your enemies as they behold you. It comes, in spite of their best efforts to conceal, because the person they swear you are is treated far better than you deserve. They are wrong in this assessment. You are never as bad as your enemies think you are, but they are right in recognition of God's favor in your life. You have been, are being, and will always be treated much better than you deserve. That's not something that says as much about you as it does about the heavenly Father you claim as your own.

3. A Bottle and a Book for Your Tears. This bold and expressive metaphor is born out of a small bottle that was often found in ancient tombs. This bottle is called a lachrymatory or a tear bottle. In the east, mourners would catch their tears in bottles (skins) and lay them at the tombs of loved ones. This was done in order to reveal to the loved ones the level of their grief and the depth of their love at separation. The path to the throne was filled with difficulties for David. God can grow a squash in a few weeks, but He takes years to grow an oak tree. God will not put a squash on a throne because it has no lasting power. Those whom God exalts to the highest positions often are given long and stern tests. Some get the answer sooner than others, but all have to endure the testing procedure. God urged David to put his tears into a bottle and record them in His book. A small girl, sick from a severe fever, crawled into her mother's lap. The girl looked up and asked her mother, "What's wrong with me?" The mother replied, "Sweetheart, I don't know, but you're going to be okay, and I'm going to stay with you and take care of you until you get better." With that assurance, the child closed her eyes and drifted off to sleep. The answer given by the mother was for the child's heart, and it was enough to comfort her in her sickness. The tear bottle was also used to comfort the sick or the troubled with a message from the heart rather than the head. If a friend or loved one was ill or in trouble, friends and family members would visit the person and take along a tear bottle with them. As the tears rolled down the face of the person who was suffering, they would be caught and bottled by the visitor to serve as a memorial of the pain endured.

David knew that God was kinder than the best family member or friend, so he asked God to bookmark and bottle his tears. David was comforted in his sorrows by having a God with a listening ear, a gentle touch, and a soothing word that knew just how to be there.

Your enemies might rejoice over your tears, but God bottles them and bookmarks them simply by being there with you. Your enemies don't know that, during those times in which they have caused you to shed tears, they have also created opportunities for greater intimacy between you and God. As God bottles your tears, He says, "I am going to stay with you and take care of you until you are better." This intimacy enables victory over subtraction. The following is a poem by Helen Keller titled "Mine to Keep":

They took away what should have been my eyes
(But I remembered Milton's Paradise)
They took away what should have been my ears
(Beethoven came and wiped away my tears)
They took away what should have been my tongue
(But I had talked with God when I was young).
He would not let them take away my soul:
Possessing that, I still possess the whole.

God will bottle your tears and bookmark your sorrows in such a way that your tears will be transmitted into triumph. Your grief will give way to a glory that will not only strengthen you but will uniquely commission you for greater works that will forever remain undefiled on the horizontal plane of history. Your enemies might create some horrible tragedies, but on the vertical plane, "Earth has no sorrow heaven cannot heal" (lyrics from "Come, Ye Disconsolate," Thomas Moore). As God bottles your tears, you will experience the kindness and tender mercies of God. You need to know that, during the sequence of all events, God draws near to His own, and the fact that He bottles our tears serves as a prophecy of a time when all tears will be removed and rewarded.

Now unto him that is able to do exceeding abundantly above all that we ask or think, according to the power that worketh in us, Unto him be glory in the church by Christ Jesus throughout all ages, world without end. Amen (Eph. 3:20-21, KJV).

As God books and bottles our tears, His power works in us through our prayers. David was praying as he asked God to "put thou my tears into thy bottle; are they not in thy book?" (Ps. 56:8, KJV) In many European cities, you can see trolleys with long poles reaching up to overhead wires and drawing down power to the engines. Neither money, methods, nor management moves the trolleys if there is no pole connecting with the overhead power. Your tears bow your knees to the Father and connect you with the power that can overcome your weakness and work mightily within you. If your enemies knew that their deeds hurt you and create a sequence of events for God to empower you, they would rush to dry your eyes before God bottles your tears.

The pain a child feels when he/she has a splinter is lessened by the attention given to him/her by his/her loving parents—who act as if nothing in the world matters more than alleviating their child's pain. To be picked up, held close, tenderly touched, softly spoken to, completely attended to, lovingly reassured that the pain will go away, and securely promised that he/she will not be left alone is a glimpse of what it means for the heavenly Father to come down from the skies and wipe the tears from your eyes and put them in His bottle. And, from the silent memory of God's book, you perform a dry-eyed bow with which He smiles upon this planet and sends forth His precious, contagious love. The destination of God's "tear bottling place" is worth whatever journey we take to reach it. The journey, however long and tedious, is inconsequential once we reach this blessed destination, where you get a glimpse of God's favor that is beyond human language to describe. Sometimes, our course is charted not by a friend who loves us but by an enemy who loathes us. We all, as Christians, get special care from God, but when we weep we get extra special care. When people or circumstances make you shed tears, it results in you being carried as opposed to being sent. It creates a closer walk, where the awesome glory of God's goodness is unveiled.

> Turn again, and tell Hezekiah the captain of my people, Thus saith the LORD, the God of David thy father, I have heard thy prayer, I have seen thy tears: behold, I will heal thee: on the third day thou shalt go up unto the house of the LORD (2 Kings 20:5, KJV).

During seasons of fragmentation and vulnerability, God gives extra special nurturing to see His servants through their periods of feebleness and injury, even if the injury leads to an isolation that is self-imposed.

> And Ahab told Jezebel all that Elijah had done, and withal how he had slain all the prophets with the sword. Then Jezebel sent a messenger unto Elijah, saying, So let the gods do to me, and more also, if I make not thy life as the life of one of them by tomorrow about this time. And when he saw that, he arose, and went for his life, and came to Beer-sheba, which belongeth to Judah, and left his servant there. But he himself went a day's journey into the wilderness, and came and sat down under a juniper tree: and he requested for himself that he might die; and said, It is enough; now, O LORD, take away my life; for I am not better than my fathers. And as he lay and slept under a juniper tree, behold, then an angel touched him, and said unto him, Arise and eat. And he looked, and, behold, there was a cake baken on the coals, and a cruse of water at his head. And he did eat and drink, and laid him down again. And the angel of the LORD came again the second time, and touched him, and said, Arise and eat; because the journey is too great for thee (1 Kings 19:1-7).

Elijah experienced both fatigue and depression. God greeted his frail hour with rest and nourishment. God's angels will show up with full hands to feed and fuel you to the next level of service just when you need it most. Jezebel's threat was not simply met with the cowardice of a prophet but with the comfort of God. Elijah left the broom tree at which he had rested and traveled to Mount Sinai—more than two hundred miles—without additional food. That angelically baked cake and cruse of water gave him extra special strength. The threat of an enemy can lead to "cakes baked on coals" in the wilderness.

After doing the very thing three times that he swore he would never do once, "Peter went out, and wept bitterly" (Luke 22:62, KJV). With the tear stains not fully dried on his face, Peter returned to familiar fishing waters and heard the voice of One who was cooking breakfast for him on the beach.

> Simon Peter saith unto them, I go a-fishing. They say unto him, We also go with thee. They went forth, and entered into a ship immediately; and that night they caught nothing. But when the morning was now come, Jesus stood on the shore: but the disciples knew not that it was Jesus. Then Jesus saith unto them, Children, have ye any meat? They answered him, No. And he said unto them, Cast the net on the right side of the ship, and ye shall find. They cast therefore, and now they were not able to draw it for the multitude of fishes. Therefore that disciple whom Jesus loved saith unto Peter, It is the LORD. Now when Simon Peter heard that it was the LORD, he girt his fisher's coat unto him, (for he was naked,) and did cast himself into the sea. And the other disciples came in a little ship; (for they were not far from land, but as it were two hundred cubits,) dragging the net with fishes. As soon then as they were come to land, they saw a fire of coals there, and fish laid thereon, and bread. Jesus saith unto them, Bring of the fish which ye have now caught. Simon Peter went up, and drew the net to land full of great fishes, and hundred and fifty and three: and for all there were so many, yet was not the net broken. Jesus saith unto them, Come and dine. And none of the disciples durst ask him, Who art thou? Knowing that it was the LORD. Jesus then cometh, and taketh bread, and giveth them, and fish likewise (John 21:3-13, KJV).

The love of Jesus cancelled the power of Peter's denial. That breakfast fire dried his eyes and serves as an affirmation that God bags our sins and bookmarks and bottles our tears.

CHAPTER III

Your Enemies Don't Know that You Can Have Good Days in Bad Times

> For he that will love life, and see good days, let him refrain his tongue from evil, and his lips that they speak no guile: Let him eschew evil, and do good; let him seek peace, and ensue it. For the eyes of the LORD are over the righteous, and his ears are open unto their prayers: but the face of the LORD is against them that do evil. And who is he that will harm you, if ye be followers of that which is good? But and if ye suffer for righteousness' sake, happy are ye: and be not afraid of their terror, neither be troubled; but sanctify the LORD God in your hearts: and be ready always to give an answer to every man that asketh you a reason of the hope that is in you with meekness and fear (1 Pet. 3:10-14, KJV).

Proverbs 16:7 says, "When a man's ways please the Lord, He maketh even his enemies to be at peace with him" (KJV). God can make your enemies set matters into motion that result in peace for you, even when they expect those matters to unravel your resolve and rock your repose. The influence your enemies might exert upon the times in which you live has little or nothing to do with the safety you can enjoy, the victories you can experience, and the goodness you can see. The morning newspaper, the state of the economy, or the shape of your stock portfolio are not the best positive points of reference to ascertain the course and color of your day. You can have good days regardless of the times in which you live. There is an ancient Hindu proverb which says, "There is nothing noble in being superior to some other man. The true nobility is in being superior to your previous self." D. L. Moody, the great evangelist of a generation ago, said, "I have had more trouble with myself than with any other man I have ever met!" Regardless of the evil spoken against you or the wickedness hurled at you, with God's help, you can work each day to correct your faults and make the most of your abilities. Each day that you labor to be "superior to your previous self" is a good day. Thomas Edison lost most of his hearing at age eight. His mother died when he was 11 years of age from the need of a simple appendectomy. The surgeons could not see well enough by candlelight to perform the procedure at night. By the time daylight arrived, it was too late. That tough time started a fire in the soul of Edison that resulted in the invention of the electric light. At age 30, Edison invented the phonograph, even though he was almost deaf. Instead of bemoaning his losses concerning his hearing, he was overheard telling someone that he considered it a blessing. When asked why, he replied, "It keeps a man honest. I can only hear loud noises, so I am told that I shout a lot. When a man has to shout and not whisper, it keeps him from telling lies because he never knows who might hear what he says." Your enemies can affect the times in which you live, but they can't sway God. The apostle Peter knew persecution from experience.

A. Threatened

And they called them, and commanded them not to speak at all nor teach in the name of Jesus. But Peter and John answered and said unto them, Whether it be right in the sight of God to hearken unto you more than unto God, judge ye. For we cannot but speak the things we have seen and heard (Acts 4:18-20, KJV).

B. Imprisoned

(And believers were the more added to the Lord, multitudes both of men and women). Insomuch that they brought forth the sick into the streets, and laid them on beds and couches, that at the least the shadow of Peter passing by might overshadow some of them. There came also a multitude out of the cities round about unto Jerusalem, bringing sick folks, and them which were vexed with unclean spirits: and they were healed every one. Then the high priest rose up, and all they that were with him, (which is the sect of the Sadducees,) and were filled with indignation, And laid their hands on the apostles, and put them in the common prison. But the angel of the Lord by night opened the prison doors, and brought them forth, and said, Go, stand and speak in the temple to the people all the words of this life. And when they heard that, they entered into the temple early in the morning, and taught. But the high priest came, and they that were with him, and called the council together, and all the senate of the children of Israel, and sent to the prison to have them brought. But when the officers came, and found them not in the prison, they returned, and told, Saying, The prison truly found we shut with all safety, and the keepers standing without before the doors: but when we had opened, we found no man within (Acts 5:14-23, KJV).

C. Beaten

Then stood there up one in the council, a Pharisee, named Gamaliel, a doctor of the law, had in reputation among all the people, and commanded to put the apostles forth a little space; And said unto them, Ye men of Israel, take heed to yourselves what ye intend to do as touching these men. For before these days rose up Theudas, boasting himself to be somebody; to whom a number of men, about four hundred, joined themselves: who was slain; and all, as many as obeyed him, were scattered, and brought to nought. After this man rose up Judas of Galilee in the days of the taxing, and drew away much people after him: he also perished; and all, even as many as obeyed him, were dispersed. And now I say unto you, Refrain from these men, and let them alone: for if this counsel or this work be of men, it will come to nought: But if it be of God, ye cannot overthrow it; lest haply ye be found even to fight against God. And to him they agreed: and when they had called the apostles, and beaten them, they commanded that they should not speak in the name of Jesus, and let them go. And they departed from the presence of the council, rejoicing that they were counted worthy to suffer shame for his name (Acts 5:34-41, KJV).

When threatened, Peter and John demonstrated the nobility of being superior to their previous selves, and that, for them, was a good day. When they were unjustly imprisoned, God sent an angel to offer hope in a seemingly unfair and harsh situation and that was a good day. How the souls of the apostles must have burned within as the heavenly messenger opened the prison doors, brought them out, and spoke to them, saying, "Go, stand and speak in the temple to the people all the words of this life" (Acts 5:20, KJV). I know that angel. I have heard his voice and seen his shining face during bad times. I have known that special hour when my eyes have widened as they bore through a bright and blinding ray of light that engulfed me at the point of my most needy times. My hands have trembled, my arms, and then my entire body as the invisible world has broken in on my bad times and strengthened me with good days. As a pastor serving one church for more than thirty years, I have had to preach eulogies of people when I would have felt more comfortable functioning as kin, sitting with their family, rather than standing behind the sacred desk, seeking to console. That angel has bound up my wounds and positioned me to shoulder my calling, and each day that it has happened has been a good day. I have seen Satan in visions, dark and ominous, stationed to land a deathblow to the ministries God has called me to embrace. I had demons dance in my sleep, and I have viewed them later defeated because of the intervention of that angel that I have spoken of. You can have good days in bad times. God will make it so. I cannot fully explain God's supernatural interventions in my life any more than the apostles could explain how they were delivered from a prison where the doors were still locked and guarded. A cursory examination of the locks, the guards, and the prison premises provided no earthly explanations.

D. Defended by Gamaliel, the Pharisee

When God is protecting you, you never can tell whom He might use to speak a word that results in support for you. Forced into a decision he could not elude, the Roman procurator Pontius Pilate faced the Lord of life with a

warning from his own wife. When others who had been ben-
eficiaries of our Lord's benevolence selected silence over
scruples, Saint Matthew shares this inspiring record:

> And Jesus stood before the governor: and the governor asked
> him, saying, Art thou the King of the Jews? And Jesus said unto
> him, Thou sayest. And when he was accused of the chief priests
> and elders, he answered nothing. Then said Pilate unto him,
> Hearest thou not how many things they witness against thee?
> And he answered him to never a word; insomuch that the gov-
> ernor marveled greatly. Now at that feast the governor was
> wont to release unto the people a prisoner, whom they would.
> And they had then a notable prisoner, called Barabbas.
> Therefore when they were gathered together, Pilate said unto
> them, Whom will ye that I release unto you? Barabbas, or Jesus
> which is called Christ? For he knew that for envy they had
> delivered him. When he was set down on the judgment seat, his
> wife sent unto him, saying, Have thou nothing to do with that
> just man: for I have suffered many things this day in a dream
> because of him (Matt. 27:11-19, KJV).

When God is protecting you, you can never tell whom He
might touch to save you in your state of defenselessness.
When the horrible conditions of slavery did not achieve
Pharaoh's evil ends in ancient Egypt, he manipulated the
persecution dial to infanticide (the killing of an infant).
Parents could not protect their newborn baby boys, but God
could not be defeated. Your enemies don't know that your
defense is never confined.

> And the Egyptians made the children of Israel to serve with
> rigour: And they made their lives bitter with hard bondage, in
> mortar, and in brick, and in all manner of service in the field: all
> their service, wherein they made them serve, was with rigour.
> And the king of Egypt spake to the Hebrew midwives, of which
> the name of the one was Shiphrah, and the name of the other
> Puah: And he said, When ye do the office of a midwife to the
> Hebrew women, and see them upon the stools; if it be a son,
> then ye shall kill him: but if it be a daughter, then she shall live.
> But the midwives feared God, and did not as the king of Egypt
> commanded them, but saved the men children alive. And the

king of Egypt called for the midwives, and said unto them,
Why have ye done this thing, and have saved the men children
alive? And the midwives said unto Pharaoh, because the
Hebrew women are not as the Egyptian women; for they are
lively, and are delivered ere the midwives come unto them.
Therefore God dealt well with the midwives: and the people
multiplied, and waxed very mighty. And it came to pass,
because the midwives feared God, that he made them houses
(Exod. 1:13-21, KJV).

God honored the faith of the midwives and protected and
rewarded them. The same God who visited Pilate's wife with
a dream that she could not dismiss and turned the hearts of
the midwives to disobey the murderous mandate of the
Egyptian king also used the flawed logic of Gamaliel to save
the lives of His faithful apostles. Gamaliel was a well-respect-
ed Pharisee who rejected our Lord. God does not have to
change the heart of your enemy in order to use him for your
good and his glory. Gamaliel was such a staunch Pharisee
that it was written, "When Rabbi Gamaliel died, the glory of
the law ceased and purity and abstinence died" (*Jewish
Talmud, Sotah* 9:15). Gamaliel was no sympathetic, open-
minded proselyte. He viewed Jesus and His movement as
one of many shooting stars that would burn out, never to be
heard from again. To undergird his argument, Gamaliel cited
the failed attempts of two insurrectionists. He recalled the
movement of a man whose name was Theudas. Theudas,
according to the elder, boasted himself "to be somebody"
and recruited a four-hundred-man army, only to drop into
the crimson sand stained with their own blood. He reminded his cohorts of one Judas of Galilee. This Judas had risen up
a revolt against Rome in about A.D. 6. Publius Sulpicius
Quirinius ordered that a census be taken to determine the tax
revenue possibility of Judea for his imperial coffers. Judas led
a revolt that was soundly crushed by the superior Roman
forces. Gamaliel advised his fellow Sanhedrin counterparts
simply to leave the apostles alone and watch their efforts
come to nothing.

It was a trying time for the apostles. Even though the majority agreed with the counsel of Gamaliel, the Law of Moses permitted flogging. This flogging involved 40 stripes save one. After receiving their 39 stripes, the apostles emerged not intimidated. The Bible teaches us that "where sin abides grace much more abides" (see Rom. 5:21) and comforts us, revealing that "greater is he that is you, than he that is in the world" (1 John 4:4, KJV). How true it is that we discover time after time that "God leads His dear children along. Some through the waters, some through the flood, Some through the fire, but all through the blood; Some through great sorrow, but God gives a song, In the night season and all the day long" ("God Leads His Dear Children Along," G. A. Young)? God's favor went to work that time, similar to the way you would take a wet towel and shake it of all its bitterness and twist from it so much pain, and we read, "And they departed from the presence of the council, rejoicing that they were counted worthy to suffer shame for his name" (Acts 5:41, KJV). That was a good day.

Phillip Brooks said, "Do not pray for easy lives. Pray to be stronger [men and women]! Do not pray for tasks equal to your powers. Pray for powers equal to your tasks." The day God gives you powers equal to your tasks is always a good day, no matter how difficult the times might appear. The special joy that the apostles felt teaches a lesson you need to learn, that your enemies can't possibly comprehend. It is a Christ-centered illustration of the fact that real joy comes not to those who seek to be happy the least but to those who seek to be faithful the most. This joy is not some object to be sought out; it is a by-product of the journey that you take. This kind of joy follows and doesn't lead. It is something that overtakes you and not something you overtake. It's not something you catch; it catches you. It's not some goal to chase; it's a benefit that will chase you. "For he that will...see good days, let him refrain his tongue from evil, and his lips that they speak no guile: Let him eschew evil, and do good; let him seek peace, and ensue it (1 Pet. 3:10-11, KJV). You don't see the good days without faithfully following the formula to refrain, to do well, and to seek peace. When you do these things, regardless of the times in which you live, you will see good days. There is a scavenger fish called the remora. The remora attaches itself to the underbelly of a shark. Attached to the underbelly of the shark, the remora doesn't have to go hunting for food. It simply hangs on to the shark and eats the scraps that fall from the shark's mouth. The joy of the Lord is inextricably fastened to faithful service. When you follow the formula of refraining, doing good, and seeking peace, no enemy's impact upon your times can impede your view of good days. Every foe that opposes you is rendered helpless in hindering your view of good days in the face of your faithfulness in God.

True nobility is being superior to "your previous self," and it is always a good day when you do so. The very worst of circumstances or times cannot rob you of the will to see a good day. Richard Wurmbrand was confined to a Romanian jail. He had no money, jewels, or material resources, but he affirmed in his heart that he would not permit his incarcerated surroundings to master him. He decided to smash the superiority of his scene and break the power of his dreary milieu. Do you know how he did it? It was not by positive thinking or systematic visualizations of open spaces. It was simple, and it was spiritual. Richard Wurmbrand decided to tithe from his prison cell. He had no money, so he gave a tithe of what he had. Every tenth day, he gave his bread rations away to prisoners more needy than himself. By tithing his bread, he made his cell into a cathedral and transformed his bread pan into an offering vessel to the glory of God. And whenever the glory of God comes into play, the day is good, in spite of the flavor of the times. Richard Wurmbrand used bread as David used water.

> And David was then in an hold, and the garrison of the Philistines was then in Bethlehem. And David longed, and said, Oh that one would give me drink of the water of the well of Bethlehem, which is by the gate! And the three mighty men brake through the host of the Philistines, and drew water out of the well of Bethlehem, that was by the gate, and took it, and brought it to David: nevertheless he would not drink thereof, but poured it out unto the Lord. And he said, Be it far from me, O Lord, that I should do this: is not this the blood of the men that went in jeopardy of their lives? therefore he would not drink it. These things did these three mighty men (2 Sam. 23:14-17, KJV).

David poured out the water he desperately desired as an offering to God because he was grateful to God for the sacrifice it represented. David refused to drink the water that his loyal, mighty men risked their lives for and transfigured a stronghold on a battlefield into a bright beacon of hallowed ground. Anything you consecrate to God, He will attend to. A crust of bread or a cup of water can trigger divine visitations, and whenever God visits His people in His glory, there is the experience of a good day.

There is a principle of dedication that works two ways. Whatever is dedicated to God is both mercifully and blessedly attended to by the Holy Spirit, and what is dedicated to Satan becomes infused with abiding evil results. When God's people advanced upon the city of Jericho, He informed them,

> And ye, in any wise keep yourselves from the accursed thing, lest ye make yourselves accursed, when ye take of the accursed thing, and make the camp of Israel a curse, and trouble it. But all the silver, and gold, and vessels of brass and iron, are consecrated unto the Lord: they shall come into the treasury of the Lord (Josh. 6:18-19, KJV).

The vessels, silver, and gold of Jericho had been dedicated to evil beings. God alone had the power to neutralize the resident evil that flowed through those instruments. The treasures of Jericho were imbued with pure evil due to the presence of demon beings. Evil has the ability to transmit itself through artifacts dedicated to the powers of darkness. Achan disobeyed God, saying, "When I saw among the spoils a goodly Babylonish garment, and two hundred shekels of silver, and a wedge of gold of fifty shekels weight, then I coveted them, and took them; and, behold, they are hid in the earth in the midst of my tent, and the silver under it" (Josh. 7:21, KJV). Thirty-six Israelite soldiers died at Ai (Josh. 7:5). The army of Israel fled in humiliation. Evil in the camp resulted in disaster. The artifact taken by Achan contained sinister results for an otherwise victorious people.

I believe that crack cocaine is a rock that was formed in the pit of hell. Crack is so powerful it can hook a person who tries it for the very first time. It destroys self-esteem and free will. It is just as much an accursed thing as the artifacts of ancient Jericho. Let no one deceive you; evil administrating its curse is a fact of life and not an example of foolish super-stition. There are some things that Satan and his demonic host have had dedicated to them that are too hot for any of us to handle. These instruments are attended to by powerful, dark forces that can penetrate any human defense system. The good news for us is there is enough power in the blood of Jesus to break any curse. What is devoted, consecrated, and humbly dedicated to God will have the life-flowing light of God's holy and all-powerful presence. The Bible informs us of that, after Solomon dedicated the Temple to God,

> That the LORD appeared to Solomon the second time, as he had appeared unto him at Gibeon. And the LORD said unto him, I have heard thy prayer and thy supplication, that thou hast made before me: I have hallowed this house, which thou hast built, to put my name there for ever; and mine eyes and mine heart shall be there perpetually (1 Kings 9:2-3, KJV).

Regardless of whether it is a costly temple, a crust of tithed bread, or a cup of water gathered at some sacrifice, when it is dedicated to God, His presence makes a place where life is redeemed and hope is renewed, and that is always a good day.

A glorious day for a gruesome time

I John, who also am your brother, and companion in tribulation, and in the kingdom and patience of Jesus Christ, was in
the isle that is called Patmos, for the word of God, and for the
testimony of Jesus Christ. I was in the Spirit on the LORD's day,
and heard behind me a great voice, as of a trumpet, Saying, I
am Alpha and Omega, the first and the last: and, What thou
seest, write in a book, and send it unto the seven churches
which are in Asia; unto Ephesus, and unto Smyrna, and unto
Pergamos, and unto Thyatira, and unto Sardis, and unto
Philadelphia, and unto Laodicea (Rev. 1:9-11, KJV).

Written history chronicles the heightening hostility of the Roman Empire toward the early Christians. John the apostle lived his last days during a period of brutal persecution. Domitian, the Roman emperor, demanded to be worshiped as a god. Christians were isolated, boycotted, and persecuted by being thrown into gladiator arenas. Some were attacked and eaten by lions. By order of the deranged emperor, some were soaked in oil and used as torches to light up the palace grounds at night. Christians were cursed, stoned, hunted, and slaughtered like wild beasts. The Christian refusal thwarted the vicious emperor's goal. Believing that God controlled history in spite of the emperor's boast that he held the fate of the world in his hands, Christians as a whole refused to forsake their Lord.

Rather than take the life of John, the government authorities had him banished to the lonely prison island of Patmos. Allied with satanic forces, this earthly power of John's last days created a wave of persecution that had, for that period, been unequalled. It was during, not after, that horrible time that God broke in. God spoke, comforted His apostle, instructed His church, undergirded His people, and revealed

His plan for earthly history and beyond. God did not leave His people to the mercy of wishful thinking. John said, "I...am your...companion in tribulation, in the kingdom and patience of Jesus Christ" (Rev. 1:9, KJV). "I was in the Spirit on the Lord's Day, and heard behind me a great voice, as of a trumpet." What a day! What a good day! What a mind-blowing, soul-stirring, hand clapping, and foot-stomping day! He saw the risen and reigning Christ. On that good and blessed day, John saw God's purpose into all eternity. Revelation 1:12, John says, "I turned to see the voice that spake with me" (KJV). I don't understand all that happened. He said, "I turned to see the voice...[and] I saw seven golden candlesticks" (KJV). I have turned to hear voices, but John was so lifted in spiritual realities that he turned to see a voice. In Solomon's book Song of Songs, Chapter 1, verse 6, there is a sad statement, which says, "They made me the keeper of vineyards; but mine own vineyard have I not kept." A man put two birds into two different bird cages. One was a sparrow, the other a canary. Both cages were placed before a sunny window. The cages were identical, and the sunshine bathed both with equal intensity. The sparrow beat its wings against the sides of the cage. It refused both food and drink. The sparrow kept alive a cry of rebellion from its cage throughout the day. The canary, different in its approach, eyed its surroundings with a quiet wisdom and open spirit; it ate and drank. It mounted the perch and filled its throat with the first effort to sing a song. At the close of the day, the sparrow lay helplessly at the bottom of its cage, battered and stained with its own blood. The canary, at the close of its day, swung and sang as it triumphed over its surroundings. Sorrow, like trouble, is a two-edged tool; it makes or mars. It can draw you closer to the place where you can hear your Father's voice of revelation or drive you to a point where hearing is eternally impaired. Rebellion never lessens suffering; it only increases your helplessness as you suffer. When you submit to God's will, even though you cannot understand it, you will triumph by laying your sorrowing soul at the feet of the One who knows just how much you can bear. When you learn to accept what God sends, you will discover that whatever He sends will prove itself to be for the best. The apostle John, in the worst of times, with no bitterness and no questions, submitted himself, and billows of peace swept over his soul from trusting in God. Your enemies can affect your times and keep some resources from knocking at your door, but they never can keep billows of peace from sweeping over your soul. Above hostile forces, God loves to speak to members of His family. He speaks today as He spoke to John on Patmos. The Roman emperor did not win when he slew the faithful any more than the Pharisees won when the Roman soldiers crucified Christ. The revelation of our Lord teaches that we are too big to find our final goal in the confines of narrow graves. A frequent Christian symbol is that of an anchor. The anchor is a symbol of hope. "We have this hope as an anchor for the soul, firm and secure" (Heb. 6:19, NIV). A Greek philosopher by the name of Epictetus said, "One must not tie a ship to a single anchor, nor life to a single hope." He was right, as long as you look at life without taking Christ into your calculations. But, through the ages, God's people have found good days in bad times, time after time, because their lives have been tied to the single hope of Jesus and His blood. Those who love Him can rejoice in the fact that He will return to vindicate the righteous and judge the wicked. Regardless of the darkness of the times, you can see good days. There is no hope of evading difficult times, but God, in His upholding grace and with His holy help, can change the inevitable into the inimitable. No enemy can stop that because no enemy can touch that.

When your enemies create bad times, say to them in your own heart, "I'll be alright because you can't stop what you can't touch." Nobody can shut down, cut out, call off, or fold up what God unfolds, transmits, and consigns. Nobody can close down, hold up, or lay off what God discloses, declares, and divulges. Nobody can terminate what God communicates. Nobody can impede what God imparts. Unwanted and unwelcome tides and times find the most worthy amongst us, but any day can become a day marked by God's favor. Follow the formula, refrain, eschew evil, do good, seek peace, and no enemy can keep you from seeing good days, even in the worst of times.

CHAPTER IV

Your Enemies Don't Know that Their Efforts to Harm Help Qualify You for Promotions Divinely Guaranteed

Then the king promoted Shadrach, Meshach and Abednego in the province of Babylon (Dan. 3:30, NIV).

There are those who are viewed as experts who state the world's best supply of perfume comes from the roses that grow exclusively in the Balkan Mountains. These roses provide a unique fragrance that must be gathered not during the daylight but in the darkest and deepest time of night. Research across the years suggests that the roses must be plucked from their thorny stalks between 12 a.m. and 2 a.m. It is during this dark interval that the blossoms give their most pleasant harvest. It is also stated that 40 percent of their fragrance disappears during the light of day. God, in His holy wisdom, determines that the work of your enemies to harm will help you by adding value to you in ways that loved ones won't. If the Chaldean enemies of Shadrach, Meshach, and Abednego had remained silent and refused to report the Hebrews refusal to the king, the promotion that came might not have come. If the Chaldeans had only ignored the young Hebrews' response to idolatry, they might have spared themselves the humiliation of becoming eyewitnesses to a higher ranking of God's people in a strange land. If the Chaldeans had simply held their peace and left these three young men alone to deal with this matter of conscience, there is a possibility that there would not have been a furnace heated seven times its normalcy for them to face and overcome. Think with me: No report, no penalty; no report, no miracle of walking through fire and

47

flames unscathed; no report, no miraculous absence of the smell of smoke; no report, no ropes severed from hand and feet; no report, no mysterious arrival and intervention of a fourth man whose form was the Son of God. The report made by the Chaldeans was full of malice and hate. It was not made to honor the law but to destroy the young leaders. The report was made to rid the land of their unwelcome competitors. But, instead of diminishing, the report made promotions possible and probable. The report meant to destroy provided a stage for the divine drama to be acted out with such power that "the king promoted Shadrach, Meshach and Abednego in the province of Babylon." This is a sweet fragrance from a dark night of the soul. If the enemies of the Hebrews had known that a promotion would come from their report, they never would have made one. I'll go a step further by saying, if they had known that the promotion would come from the report, they not only would have kept silent, they would have made sure everybody else kept their mouths shut as well. If they had known that the fiery furnace would end up becoming a victory circle for God's people, they would have tried to put the fire out rather than watch its heat index rise higher and higher.

Like the Chaldeans, much of what your enemies think is just not true. Mark Twain once quipped, "It ain't what you don't know that gets you into trouble. It's what you know for sure that just ain't so." Most of us were told that Cinderella's slipper was made of glass, and we passed it on unexamined. The truth is that the slipper Cinderella lost was not made of glass but of ermine. When the story was translated from its original French language into English, the word for ermine was mistaken for the similar word for glass. Misinformation is responsible for Cinderella having to cram her feet into those uncomfortable glass slippers. Your enemies think that the trouble they send will destroy you. They are wrong. Trouble rightly borne will mature you, bless you, enlarge you, and elicit the best from you. Trouble rightly confronted will make you more valuable. The Bible tells us that, prior to the fiery furnace incident, the king "in all matters of wisdom and understanding...found [the Hebrew boys] ten times better than all the magicians and astrologers that were in all his realm" (Dan. 1:20, KJV). However, "wisdom and understanding" is one thing, but walking unharmed through fiery flames demonstrates worth and value at a far more significant level. The fiery furnace incident spoke of power beyond "wisdom and understanding." Wisdom and understanding can reveal evil, but evil exposed is not the same thing as evil expelled and overcome. The disapproval of the men whose report removed the Hebrews was overruled by the approval of their God, who raised their stock. The king's assessment essentially stated that these men were too valuable to remain at their then-present levels, and the king promoted them to greater seats of authority. One day soon, we shall all see God's proneness to secure a mighty harvest during the deep and dark seasons of our nights.

An artist painted a boat loaded with cattle. The cattle were being ferried across a swollen river during the time of a fierce storm. The dark, ominous clouds amalgamated with treacherous and jagged lighting bolts created a picture of cattle marked for destruction. However, destruction was not their plight. The artist named the picture "Changing for Better Pastures." Beloved, we are from time to time prone to stay with the familiar pastures that we've grown accustomed to. Friends and family concerned about our comfort might be unwilling to move us, but enemies who care not for our comfort or complaints will try to move us out of comfort zones. God might not intervene and cease the journey, but He will mandate that it becomes a "Changing for Better Pastures." Never permit the journey to rush you to make premature and erroneous conclusions about the destination. The crossing might not be smooth, but the destination is always safe.

A. God Can Find Islands in the Fog

And we being exceedingly tossed with a tempest, the next day they lightened the ship; And the third day we cast out with our own hands the tackling of the ship. And when neither sun nor stars in many days appeared, and no small tempest lay on us, all hope that we should be saved was then taken away. But after long abstinence Paul stood forth in the midst of them, and said, Sirs, ye should have hearkened unto me, and not have loosed from Crete, and to have gained this harm and loss. And now I exhort you to be of good cheer: for there shall be no loss any man's life among you, but of the ship. For there stood by me this night the angel of God, whose I am, and whom I serve, Saying, Fear not, Paul; thou must be brought before Caesar: and, lo, God hath given thee all them that sail with thee. Wherefore, sirs, be of good cheer: for I believe God, that it shall be even as it was told me. Howbeit we must be cast upon a certain island (Acts 27:18-26, KJV).

The Bible records how God kept His Word in verse 44 "and the rest, some on boards, and some on broken pieces of the ship. And so it came to pass, that they escaped all safe to land." The journey was difficult at times. They banded the ship, which meant they passed ropes under and over the ship to hold the ship together, but their best efforts failed. The angry storm raged unabated for days. The sun and stars were blotted out, and this meant the loss of hope for many. Ships in Paul's day had no compasses and had to be navigated by the stars. With the stars blotted out, the ship was driven across the Adriatic Sea at the mercy of providence. God was good, and as the unseen pilot on a storm-tossed sea, He safely landed the vessel on an island, in spite of the fog. "And when they were escaped, then they knew that the island was called Melita" (Acts 28:1, KJV).

This scripture has a special meaning for me. In 1967, I was a young United States Air Force sergeant stationed at Goose Bay, Labrador, in Canada. The evening sun set with our small fishing boat located miles away from our port. To make matters worse, we spied a Russian warship, which meant that we had somehow drifted beyond neutral waters. We couldn't crank our motor out of fear of detection. I cannot explain how it happened, but at 10:15 p.m., our boat hit something in the water! When we gathered our senses, we found that what we had hit was our own harbor. I cannot recall the incident without wanting to shout out "worthy is the Lamb of God." I know that God can see in the dark, and He always knows where the right harbor is. Children of God, we serve one who can find islands in the fog, harbors in the dark, and a refuge in the worst of storms.

There is a Jewish tradition that relates. It's a story titled "The Two Angels." According to the tradition, after Adam fell from his state of grace, God sent two angels from heaven together to deal with humankind's sinful nature. One angel was named Judgment, and the other was called Mercy. The two angels' work will continue until the race of humankind is ultimately separated, judged, and redeemed. Where one angel afflicts, the other angel heals. Where one uproots, the other plants a flower. Where one craves a wrinkle, the other kindles a smile. Where one creates a storm, the other brings a rainbow. Unbidden, sometimes, mercy calls in the night and points the way to safe havens. It is a way no soul can discover for itself and yet, in the process of that revelation, the soul finds its worth increased above measure.

B. The Lie that Unlocked the Door for a Promotion

And it came to pass about this time, that Joseph went into the house to do his business; and there was none of the men of the house there within. And she caught him by his garment, saying, Lie with me: and he left his garment in her hand, and fled, and got him out. And it came to pass, when she saw that he had left his garment in her hand, and was fled forth, That she called unto the men of her house, and spake unto them, saying, See, he hath brought in an Hebrew unto us to mock us; he came in unto me to lie with me, and I cried with a loud voice: And it came to pass, when he heard that I lifted up my voice and cried, that he left his garment with me, and fled, and got him out. And she laid up his garment by her, until his lord came home. And she spake unto him, according to these words, saying, The Hebrew servant, which thou hast brought unto us, came in unto me to mock me: And it came to pass, as I lifted up my voice and cried, that he left his garment with me, and fled out. And it came to pass, when his master heard the words of his wife, which she spake unto him, saying, After this manner did thy servant to me; that his wrath was kindled. And Joseph's master took him, and put him into the prison, a place where the king's prisoners were bound: and he was there in the prison (Gen. 39:11-20, KJV).

There are no documents that suggest Joseph would have met the king's butler, who gave Joseph a way into the king's palace, if he had remained a steward over Potiphar's household. There are no records that summon up any set of circumstances whereby Joseph might have made his entry into the palace without an exit from the king's prison. It was Potiphar's wife's lie that landed Joseph in the king's prison, where he met the butler. Without the lie, Joseph might have lived and died without becoming a ruler in Egypt second only to Pharaoh. Without the lie, it is possible that Joseph's ability to interpret dreams might have diminished due to a lack of use. There are no reasons to believe that anybody in Potiphar's house had any dreams that ever needed to be interpreted. Without the lie, Joseph would not have learned what God could do in prison. Without the lie, Joseph would not have gained the administration experience.

But the LORD was with Joseph, and shewed him mercy, and gave him favour in the sight of the keeper of the prison. And the keeper of the prison committed to Joseph's hand all the prisoners that were in the prison; and whatsoever they did there, he was the doer of it. The keeper of the prison looked not to any thing that was under his hand; because the LORD was with him, and that which he did, the LORD made it to prosper (Gen. 39:21-23, KJV).

The prison experience made Joseph into a more valuable person, transformed him into a public servant, and apparently healed him of his inexperienced behavior of telling his dreams to non-dreamers. Joseph's prison experience reveals clearly how God used a lie as a vehicle in which Joseph received a promotion.

Martin Luther had a close friend by the name of John Brentz. During the reformation, Brentz incurred the intense hatred of King Charles V. The king made several attempts to kill him. Hearing that an army of Spanish cavalry men was on its way to arrest him, Brentz went into prayer. The Spirit of God spoke to him, saying, "Take a loaf of bread and go into the upper town and where thou findest a door open, enter and hide thyself under the roof." John Brentz obeyed the heavenly mandate. He found the only door that was open and hid himself in the loft. For 14 days, he hid as the Spanish army searched for him in vain. The one loaf of bread would have proven to be insufficient, but day by day, a hen came up into the loft and laid an egg without cackling. On the 15th day, the hen didn't show up. John heard on that day the people rejoicing as they sang, "They are gone at last! Praise God, they are gone at last!" He went down and found the army gone. The same God who fed His servant with eggs laid by a hen that didn't cackle also promoted His servant, Joseph, through a lie that put him in prison. The same God who makes the rooster crow can keep an egg-laying hen from cackling.

The Golden Gate Bridge connecting Northern California to San Francisco remains one of the most spectacular bridges in the world. There are two massive towers located 1,125 feet apart. These towers hold two thirty-six-and-a-half inch cables from which the bridge is suspended. The six-lane bridge was completed in April 1937 at a cost of $36.7 million. During the first phase of construction, there were no safety nets beneath the workers. Eleven men fell to their deaths during one accident. During the second phase of construction, a safety net was installed. Nineteen men's lives were saved because, even though they fell, the net caught and held them. The work was done at a 25 percent faster pace. The workmen had the assurance that, if they fell, they would not perish. Even though your enemies might design plans for your demise, God is faithful. Goodness and mercy are tracking you. You might be the object of false reports, ridicule, and brazen attacks, but God is faithful. It is not God's will that you simply get by. He wants to promote you, and He loves to do it in ways that reveal His greatness. If you give God your difficult cases, you will discover the glory of His goodness and the fulfillment of His promises. The dew might sparkle, the flowers might bloom while fountains mesmerized with their glory, but nothing compares to the eternal glory that radiates from our God as He overcomes our difficult cases and vicious enemies. There are some challenging lessons for us to learn, and one of the hardest is that, while our Father's nature is love, even for those who serve Him most faithfully, there is no immunity from trial. God has not promised us exemption from sorrow but, rather, triumph in it. "In the world ye shall have tribulation" says our Lord, "but be of good cheer; I have overcome the world" (John 16:33b, KJV).

> For ye have need of patience, that, after ye have done the will of God, ye might receive the promise. For yet a little while, and he that shall come will come, and will not tarry (Heb. 10:36-37, KJV).

Joseph was only 17 years old when he arrived in Egypt. He spent 11 years in Potiphar's house as a slave-steward. His master's wife's lie sent him to the king's prison. He was even forgotten by the butler that he befriended, but he was patient.

The person who wrote the epistle to the Hebrews was aware of the trials and tests that beset the Church of his day. The Roman Empire sought to annihilate Christians. The faith of new believers was being challenged on a daily basis. The Temple at Jerusalem was either destroyed or was about to be destroyed. Some might have wondered about the wisdom of praying but not the writer of Hebrews. He stood firm. He held out. He claimed our Lord's promises. His words echoed an amazing confidence: God heard. God responded, and He always will. Your enemies don't know it, but God can and will use their harmful efforts to help you qualify for the very promotions that He has promised.

The veiled path of promotion for Joseph was a lie, which landed him in the king's prison. The cryptic trail for the three Hebrew youths was the fiery furnace. The Bible informs us of our personal need to remain focused and to work in the spirit of excellence. "Whatsoever thy hand findeth to do, do it with thy might" (Eccl. 9:10, KJV). "Seest thou man diligent in his business? he shall stand before kings; he shall not stand before mean men" (Prov. 22:29, KJV). "Withhold not good from them to whom it is due, when it is in the power of thine hand to do it" (Prov. 3:27, KJV). "The soul of the sluggard desireth, and hath nothing: but the soul of the diligent shall be made fat" (Prov. 13:4, KJV). "Follow peace with all men, and holiness, without which no man shall see the Lord" (Heb. 12:14, KJV). "But foolish and unlearned questions avoid, knowing that they do gender strifes. And the servant of the Lord must not strive; but be gentle unto all men, apt to teach, patient" (2 Tim. 2:23-24, KJV).

All men will not follow peace with you, but you can follow peace with them. You are not responsible for what is in someone's heart toward you, but you are responsible for what is in your heart toward others. Don't give Satan a stronghold in your life; forgive others unasked. Work hard, and work smart. Give God your problems without giving God a deadline, and failure in one place will sow the seeds for a promotion in another.

Abraham Lincoln knew failure long before he enjoyed success. Lincoln's passage of promotion included one failure after another.

- Defeated for legislature - 1832
- Second failure in business - 1833

- Suffered depression - 1836
- Defeated for Speaker - 1838
- Defeated for election - 1840
- Defeated for Congress - 1848
- Defeated for Senate -1855
- Defeated for Vice President - 1856
- Defeated for Senate - 1858
- Elected President - 1860

With God's help, nothing is impossible to a soul that is open and willing. There is no power, be it man, horse, financial, political, demonic, psychic, angelic, atomic, microscopic, telescopic, military, or nuclear that can measure up to the omnipotent power of God. God submits to no superior, answers to no authority, and reports to no ruler. No obstruction can block God. No adversity can hinder God. No circumstance can constrain God; no situation can restrict God. What God promises, God performs.

> Blessed shalt thou be when thou comest in, and blessed shalt thou be when thou goest out. The LORD shall cause thine enemies that rise up against thee to be smitten before thy face: they shall come out against thee one way, and flee before thee seven ways (Deut. 28:6-7, KJV).

Don't live beneath your privileges. Despite the threats and even violence that you might have to endure, make your trusting heart God's home. If you will do so, heaven will grant you a strong and steely conviction concerning the victory that will be achieved. Go to bed each night resting on God's resolve to promote you, and wake up each day expecting Him to bring it to pass.

Despite the lies and the liars, lift up your eyes unto the hills and say, "I have chosen the way of truth: thy judgments have I laid before me. I have stuck unto thy testimonies: O Lord, put me not to shame" (Ps. 119:30-31, KJV).

The young Hebrews were groomed for high office. Their intelligence had secured for them some impressive prospects. Joseph was surrounded by paganism on every side in Egypt. The Hebrews could have followed the lead of their peers and said "yes" to the world, but instead, they chose to say "yes" to the Word. Joseph could have compromised his convictions in Potiphar's house, but he chose the path of peril that God transformed into the path of promotion. The common thread holding each of them was a choice made to tempt the wrath of flesh and blood rather than set aside the law of God.

The psalmist understood that common conviction, and he said, "I have stuck unto thy testimonies: O Lord, put me not to shame." The word *stuck* is self explanatory. It means "to be attached." It does not mean that one is stuck with something but stuck to something. God's testimonies were no burdens for the psalmist to weep over. They were anchors that he chose to stick himself to. In other words, he had glued himself to the Word and rule of God, and nothing could pry him loose. Your enemies don't know what you are stuck to. They might deride you, but they can't pry you loose. Let them plan, plot, scheme, back bite, and slander you; pay them no mind because God won't let you down.

Promotions promised are promotions guaranteed. Your enemies will be able to stop you when they are able to stop God. Your enemies will be able to defeat you on the day after they defeat God. During the reformation, Martin Luther had periods of depression. On one occasion, his wife noticed an increase in duration. She went into her closet, dressed up in black, and put a veil over her face. As she moved about the house, he noticed her dress attire and asked, "Who died?" She responded, "God. He must be dead; otherwise, you would not be as depressed as you are." Her statements shook the reformer out of his depression and sent him out with a new fire in his soul as he preached "The Just Shall Live by Faith." Love, live, work, and serve like you believe God lives. Make your choices like you know it is so.

CHAPTER V

Your Enemies Don't Know that Every Hit They Inflict on You Is Out of Bounds

So they hanged Haman on the gallows that he had prepared for Mordecai. Then was the king's wrath pacified (Est. 7:10, KJV).

A. Negotiated Treachery Is Out of Bounds

Haman the Agagite hatched an expensive plot to wipe out Mordecai and the Jews, but his efforts proved to be futile. In the game of football, if you are on defense and you tackle or hit an offensive player out of bounds, two things happen. First of all, the hit doesn't count against the person hit, and secondly, you get penalized for the hit. If the hit is really outrageous, you could, as Haman did, get thrown out of the game entirely. Either way, if you're on defense, you hurt yourself when you hit somebody out of bounds. If you are on offense and you make a one-handed, sensational catch out of bounds, it doesn't count. It is meaningless unless, of course, some defensive player from your opponent's team is foolish enough to hit you out of bounds.

Haman the Agagite was a lifelong enemy of the Jews. He was a descendant of the Amalekites. Planted by providence in the Book of 1 Samuel, there is a costly story concerning disobedience. God had commanded Saul, Israel's first king, to kill the Amalekites. These Amalekites had been enemies of God's people, evidenced by the attack upon them during their exodus from Egypt. Saul refused to obey God. He spared King Agag. The Agagites, descendants of a ruthless Amalekite people, were offspring King Saul refused to kill. Evil escalated, and in the Book of Esther, Haman the Agagite put in motion an anti-semitic extermination plan.

Haman abused the position given to him by the favor of King Ahasuerus. He advanced a proposition where he was willing to pay approximately twenty million dollars to cover the cost of his genocidal program. Appealing to the king's superstitious beliefs and greed, Haman pressed the right buttons and pulled the right strings. Using the king's signet ring to seal his wicked plans, he had a decree written that was designed to destroy all of the Jews in the Persian Empire. He even set the date on the 13th day of the Jewish month of Adar. The document was binding. It could not be nullified or reversed. Haman instructed that a gallows 70 feet high be built in order to see Mordecai, the Jew, dangling from the end of a rope. The plan seemed flawless. Every contingency seemed to be anticipated.

Haman had money, power, and troops. He knew how to manipulate the systems of his day. The problem with Haman's treachery was that it was all out of bounds. God alone draws the lines within which we must operate. No plan, no power, and no potentate can cross what God labels as uncrossable without consequences.

In the game of baseball, the field of play is divided by what is fair and what is foul. A batter can hit a foul ball 500 feet, but it doesn't count. When the ball is foul, whether it's a line drive or a towering shot, it still is out of bounds. In basketball, when a foul is made and the fouling team has made the penalty, the person fouled gets a chance to make free throws without running time off the clock. Children of God, Satan's team makes the penalties. He is a defeated foe. In the story of Haman, the Jews were behind. They only had eight months and 10 days. God stepped into the king's dream. God gave Queen Esther His favor and allowed Haman to be caught in a position in the queen's presence that moved the king to have Haman hanged on the very gallows that he had built, upon which he intended to have hanged Mordecai. God gave Esther Haman's household and had another decree written authorizing the Jews to arm themselves. The day of reckoning became a day of celebration. In the city of Shushan, the Jews slew five hundred of their enemies and three hundred more in the adjoining countryside. Some seventy-five thousand enemy troops fell before their swords, and a day scheduled for mourning became a day of celebration. The 10 sons of Haman were slain. Mordecai was dressed in Haman's robes before Haman was hanged, and Haman watched as Mordecai was honored before the nation—talk about being penalized!

Today, the Jews gladly celebrate God's mighty intervention during the days of Esther and Mordecai with the "feast of Purim." The ninth chapter of Esther informs us that Haman selected the 13th day of Adar as the day of the destruction of the Jews by casting a lot called a *pur*. The Jews called the celebration "Purim after the Pur."

God could have prevented the acts of Haman, but He chose to teach us that negotiated treachery is out of bounds. And, while out of bounds difficulties can't defeat us, they can create serious penalties for those who hit us. When enemies plan and plot, Jesus Christ is still the real and practical power in God's business on this earth. He not only justifies the Law, but He is a victorious companion for every rough road. Your enemies might laugh and brag about the hits they inflict, but all of their hits fall out of bounds.

1. God can give back years lost.

And I will restore to you the years that the locust hath eaten, the cankerworm, and the caterpillar, and the palmerworm, my great army which I sent among you (Joel 2:25, KJV).

2. God can make time go back.

And Hezekiah said unto Isaiah, What shall be the sign that the LORD will heal me, and that I shall go up into the house of the LORD the third day? And Isaiah said, This sign shalt thou have of the LORD, that the LORD will do the thing that he hath spoken: shall the shadow go forward ten degrees, or go back ten degrees? And

Hezekiah answered, It is a light thing for the shadow to go down ten degrees: nay, but let the shadow return backward ten degrees. And Isaiah the prophet cried unto the LORD: and he brought the shadow ten degrees backward, by which it had gone down in the dial of Ahaz (2 Kings 20:8-11, KJV).

3. God can make time stand still.

Then spake Joshua to the LORD in the day when the LORD delivered up the Amorites before the children of Israel, and he said in the sight of Israel, Sun, stand thou still upon Gibeon; and thou, Moon, in the valley of Ajalon. And the sun stood still, and the moon stayed, until the people had avenged themselves upon their enemies. Is not this written in the book of Jasher? So the sun stood still in the midst of heaven, and hasted not to go down about a whole day. And there was no day like that before it or after it, that the Lord hearkened unto the voice of a man: for the Lord fought for Israel (Josh. 10:12-14, KJV).

On April 18, 1521, Martin Luther stood at the Diet of Worms. Facing death threats and charges of heresy, he said, "Here I stand, I can do no other. God help me. Amen." The Roman church officials hated him, but he went forth, declaring, "The just shall live by faith." God stood with him, and every hit inflicted upon the Protestant Reformation fell out of bounds.

In Birmingham, Alabama, during the early 1960s, Dr. Martin Luther King, Jr., wrote "Agape love is love seeking to preserve and create community. Love is a willingness to go to any length to restore community. The cross is the eternal expression of the extent to which God will go in order to restore broken community. The resurrection is a symbol of God's triumph over all the forces that seek to block community. The Holy Spirit is the continuing community, creating reality that moves through history." Bull Connors, of the KKK, and a host of others aligned themselves against Martin Luther King, Jr., but God decreed their evil deeds to be hits inflicted out of bounds. Dr. King lives beyond his grave because God ruled the works of his enemies to be out of bounds. They hit him. They even killed him, but they didn't stop him because out of bounds hits don't count against the person being hit.

Wilson Johnson is the founder of Holiday Inn® motels. His story is a wonderful example of God's unlimited and amazing grace. At the age of 40, Mr. Johnson worked in a sawmill. One morning, due to no fault of his own, he was fired. He felt that his world had caved in on him, but by the grace of God, he fought off his depression. He mortgaged his home and went into the construction business. Within five years, he became a multimillionaire. He stated, on one occasion, "At the time I was fired, I didn't understand it. Later, however, I saw that it was God's unerring and wonderful plan to get me into the way of His choosing." The Bible informs us clearly that God "breathed into [Adam's] nostrils the breath of life; and man became a living soul" (Gen. 2:7, KJV). The same God is able and willing to breathe a new breath into a life that feels that life is over. And, time after time, God flexes His divine muscles by blessing us through the penalties passed upon those who hit us out of bounds with treachery. How privileged we are, even as treachery unmercifully assaults us, that we can support our spirits, saying,

> For we have not an high priest which cannot be touched with the feeling of our infirmities; but was in all points tempted like as we are, yet without sin. Let us therefore come boldly unto the throne of grace, that we obtain mercy, and find grace to help in time of need (Heb. 4:15-16, KJV).

The Bible does not minimize treachery, nor does it overemphasize its power. David saw it for what it was.

> The wicked plotteth against the just, and gnasheth upon him with his teeth. The LORD shall laugh at him: for he seeth that his day is coming. The wicked have drawn out the sword, and have bent their bow, to cast down the poor and needy, and to slay such as be of upright conversation. Their sword shall enter into their own heart, and their bows shall be broken (Ps. 37:12-15, KJV).

I know of no greater penalty for treachery than for the offenders' swords to enter into their own hearts. God's grace is truly astonishing as it exceeds all of our reasoning, astounding as it ministers to all of our needs, and abounding as it satisfies our greatest requirements.

In the Congo, a father called to his son. The boy was in a garden, playing under a tree. The father said, "Obey me now; get down on your stomach." The boy obeyed. The father then said, "Crawl to me quickly." The boy obeyed again without debate. As he crawled toward his father, the father spoke to his son again, saying, "Stand up and run to me." The boy reached his father. The father picked him up and turned him around. To his surprise, the boy saw a sixteen foot snake hanging from the limb of the tree he had been playing under. The father saw the danger the boy wasn't aware of. The directives to fall to the ground, crawl, and run came with no explanations. The child never asked, "Why?" He simply obeyed. The child moved beyond the threat because he had the wisdom to obey his father's voice without wasting time requesting explanations. God will speak when necessary. Don't question Him; simply obey. You never know what He is calling you out of. When you can't see His hand, you can always trust His heart. When things pile up or fall apart, even though you might not see the light at the end of the tunnel, God does. Demanding nothing in return but our love, God shoulders the loads, shares the chaos, and tunnels a way out. People can be treacherous, but God will decree the treachery to be out of bounds, and therefore, it becomes a clawless and toothless beast without the strength of a newborn kitten.

B. Name Calling Is Out of Bounds

In Shakespeare's *Romeo and Juliet*, Juliet asked Romeo an important question.

"What's in a name? That which we call a rose, by any other word would smell as sweet." Juliet's answer was right, but name-calling can hurt. If name-calling didn't hurt, Jacob would never have renamed the second son he had with his beloved Rachel.

> And they journeyed from Bethel; and there was but a little way to come to Ephrath: and Rachel travailed, and she had hard labour. And it came to pass, when she was in hard labour, that the midwife said unto her, Fear not; thou shalt have this son also. And it came to pass, as her soul was in departing, (for she died) that she called his name Benoni: but his father called him Benjamin (Gen. 35:16-18, KJV).

The name *Benoni* means "son of my sorrow." The name *Benjamin* means "son of my right hand." The name of Jesus makes name-calling out of bounds because there is so much right about Jesus' name that it compensates for anything wrong with any other name. The apostle Paul instructs us on this reality:

> Wherefore God also hath highly exalted him, and given him a name which is above every name: That at the name of Jesus every knee should bow, of things in heaven, and things in earth, and things under the earth; And that every tongue should confess that Jesus Christ is Lord, to the glory of God the Father (Phil. 2:9-11, KJV).

Jesus is the New Testament Greek name of the Old Testament Hebrew name Joshua. Both names mean "the Lord is salvation." In the Old Testament, God's presence was banned from humankind because of Adam's sin. In the New Testament, God's presence is made available through Jesus/Joshua because He broke the curse. Let no person "cuss" or "curse" you with out of bounds name-calling. The name of Jesus means "the Lord is salvation." It means all kinds of salvation—physical, mental, spiritual, financial, and many other forms. Jesus is the last Adam and the second man.

> And so it is written, The first man Adam was made a living soul; the last Adam was made a quickening spirit. Howbeit that

was not first which is spiritual, but that which is natural; and afterward that which is spiritual. The first man is of the earth, earthy: the second man is the LORD from heaven (1 Cor. 15:45-47, KJV).

He that cometh from above is above all: he that is of the earth is earthly, and speaketh of the earth: he that cometh from heaven is above all (John 3:31, KJV).

Jesus is not called the last man but the second man. As the second man, He is the origin of a new humanity, the head of a new race of born-again believers. He is the last Adam to come, the last Adam needed to mend what the first Adam lost. He is the last Adam vital in the universal refurnishing of that which the first Adam summarily repulsed.

As the last Adam and the second man, Jesus remains Lord from heaven and He that is above all. Your enemies will seek to ill name and rename you because they don't know that you have a name that is above all, superior to all, higher than all, and beyond the defeat of all. When you greet the names enemies give you in and with the name of Jesus, you dethrone any power to adversely affect your victory. Let them call you incompetent, foolish, criminal, loser, and liar. Speak Jesus to the name! You can't unbite where a snake has bitten or unring once a bell has been rung, but you can speak the name that makes the name-calling out of bounds. And, remember, when something is out of bounds, it can't impede your victory. The writer of Proverbs instructs us, saying,

A GOOD name is rather to be chosen than great riches, and loving favour rather than silver and gold (Prov. 22:1, KJV).

We all desire to have a good name, but some of us go wrong because we worship our good name as if it is some kind of God. Moses was easily at the top of Pharaoh's most wanted list, and he was not called a prophet or liberator. Ahab and Jezebel never would have written the prophet Elijah a positive letter of reference. When John the Baptist burst upon the Judean landscape as "a voice crying in the wilderness," he was so hated that he was beheaded and his head placed on a platter to appease the pagan resentment of the wife of King Herod.

> For John the Baptist came neither eating bread nor drinking wine; and ye say, He hath a devil. The Son of man is come eating and drinking; and ye say, Behold a gluttonous man, and a winebibber, a friend of publicans and sinners! (Luke 7:33-34, KJV).

Our Lord refused to be intimidated by the name-calling. Although He was criticized for healing on the Sabbath, He continued to heal the lame, bless the lost, raise up the fallen, receive the confessions of the repentant, and, with open arms, embrace the lepers. There was so much right with the name of Jesus that it nullified the charges inherent in the names assigned to Him by His enemies, such as gluttonous, winebibber, and friend of publicans and sinners. "Jesus stands erect amid the fallen, clean amid the defiled, living among the dying, the Savior of all humankind." George Matheson once said, "Son of man, whenever I doubt of life, I think of thee. Nothing is so impossible as that Thou shouldst be dead. I can imagine the hills to dissolve into vapor, the stars to melt in smoke, and the rivers to empty themselves in sheer exhaustion, but I felt no limit in Thee." There is no limit in Christ. The glory of this deity bursts forth at His discretion. No word spoken against you can prevail as long as you fasten yourself securely to the Rock that can't be moved.

There is an aged story that concerns itself with a traveler in ancient Greece who had lost his way and, seeking to find it, sought directions from a man by the roadside, who later turned out to be Socrates. The lost man asked, "How can I reach Mt. Olympus?" To this man's request, Socrates is reported to have said, "Just make every step you take go in that direction." When a soul is able to keep his eye on his God-given goal and not waste time and energy answering name-callers, he is "well on the way to his own Mt. Olympus, however modest his particular peak may be."

> Be not afraid of sudden fear, neither of the desolation of the
> wicked, when it cometh. For the LORD shall be thy confidence,
> and shall keep thy foot from being taken (Prov. 3:25-26, KJV).

C. Needling Mockery Is Out of Bounds

Mockery has defeated some people that the most severe threats have left impassive and immovable. Some whose courage has stood the onslaught of savage beasts and ruthless men have found their spirits unable to summon defiance in the presence of those obstacles created by mockery. Some whose cries have broken the slumber of nations have found their voices muted by the needling sneers that flew from the lips of mockers.

Mockery is defined as "scornful derision" or "ridicule." It can be in the form of a false, derisive, or impudent imitation. It can also be something ludicrously unsuitable or fertile. More often than not, mockery means to be laughed at. It is being made fun of. It is a sacrilege of what you hold sacred. It is a bludgeoning of raw self-esteem and nerves. It is a put-down of what you put way up. It is a deviling of what you love.

Your enemies mock you in order to hurt you. They don't know their mockery only has power to pain in direct proportion to your willingness to allow mockery to cause pain. Satan views mockery as a powerful instrument to use, and he employs it through your enemies to stop you short of your mission. The Bible, however, views mockery as a foul that the divine Referee will call every time it is committed. The reason for this is simple; mockery is a sin against Him—a foul, if you will, that is aimed at the Creator.

> Whoso mocketh the poor reproacheth his Maker: and he that is
> glad at calamities shall not be unpunished (Prov. 17:5, KJV).

Mocking the poor is mocking the God who made them. Mocking the weak is mocking the Creator who keeps them. Mocking any person results in ridiculing the God who formed them, framed them, and fuels them. Job was so aware of the penalty for the sin of mockery that he cited it as a sin he carefully avoided, even as he viewed the fate of his enemies.

> This also were an iniquity to be punished by the judge: for I should have denied the God that is above. If I rejoice at the destruction of him that hated me, or lifted up myself when evil found him: Nether have I suffered my mouth to sin by wishing a curse to his soul (Job 31:28-30, KJV).

The mocker is living in out-of-bounds territory every time he mocks you. Proverbs says, "He that is glad at calamities shall not be unpunished" (Prov. 17:5, KJV).

1. The mockers want to stop you. Don't let them.

> But it came to pass, that when Sanballat heard that we builded the wall, he was wroth, and took great indignation, and mocked the Jews. And he spake before his brethren and the army of Samaria, and said, What do these feeble Jews? will they fortify themselves? will they sacrifice? will they make an end in a day? will they revive the stones out of the heaps of rubbish which are burned? Now Tobiah the Ammonite was by him, and he said, Even that which they build, if a fox go up, he shall even break down their stone wall. Hear, O our God; for we are despised: and turn their reproach upon their own head, and give them for a prey in the land of captivity: And cover not their iniquity, and let not their sin be blotted out from before thee: for they have provoked thee to anger before the builders. So built we the wall; and all the wall was joined together unto the half thereof: for the people had a mind to work (Neh. 4:1-6, KJV).

Mockery can cut deeply, if you let it. Nehemiah met the mockery of Sanballat and Tobiah with prayer. He didn't debate with them. He didn't trade insults. He didn't defend the quality of their builders' workmanship or the skills of their craftsmen. The hymn goes, "Just tell Jesus, tell Him all." Nehemiah didn't allow the mockers to succeed because he did not engage them. When you are trading insults with your enemies, they are winning. Keep your focus on your God-given assignment. Keep running. Stay in your lane. If there is any fouling to be done, let it be by them. The foul might not be called into your hearing when it is committed, but it is called, and the divine Judge will enforce the penalty according to His schedule.

On October 16, 1995, the Million Man March was held in the nation's capital. There were scores of people who said it would not, could not, and should not take place, but it did. Organizers defined the event as "a day of atonement and unity for Black men" nationwide. There were many mockers, and the mockery was, at times, quite mean-spirited. Those present pledged themselves to take greater responsibility for themselves and their families. Some stated that the day signified the further reawakening of the sense of unity, purpose, efficacy, and self-worth of black men. Some psychologists labeled it as "A Black Holy Day." The march was a good thing that happened despite the fact the mockers said it would never happen. It happened because organizers kept focused, worked hard, and refused to succumb to out-of-bounds insults.

Mother's Day is the third most celebrated holiday in the world. Only Christmas and Easter are more publicly celebrated. Mother's Day was started by Anna M. Jarvis. Miss Jarvis was one of 12 siblings and one of the four children who lived to see adulthood. Her mother died in 1905. Miss Jarvis dedicated the rest of her life working to set aside a special day to honor mothers. She made speeches, wrote thousands of letters, and traveled countless miles. Many felt that she was wasting her time. It was not until May 10, 1908, three years after her mother's death, that she organized the first Mother's Day celebration. It was held at the Andrews Methodist Church in Grafton, West Virginia. It was not until 1914 that President Woodrow Wilson proclaimed that the second Sunday in May should be celebrated as Mother's Day. Whatever God considers worth giving you to do, Satan considers worth opposing, and mockery is one of his tools.

Mockery has a way of confronting us at the point of our weaknesses. You can become so accustomed to managing your life that, when the unmanageable comes along, you panic. There is a wonderful event in the 14th chapter of Genesis. Abraham had defeated four well-armed kings. After the battle, fear began to mock him, and he began to worry about a rematch. During his sleep, God appeared to him and strengthened him, saying, "Fear not, Abram: I am thy shield, and thy exceeding great reward" (Gen. 15:1, KJV). Enemies might be large, and walls might be high, but God is above them all. Mockers want to stop you. Don't let them.

2. The mockers want to dissuade you. Don't assist them.

While he yet spake, there came from the ruler of the synagogue's house certain which said, Thy daughter is dead: why troublest thou the Master any further? As soon as Jesus heard the word that was spoken, he saith unto the ruler of the synagogue, be not afraid, only believe. And he suffered no man to follow him, save Peter, and James, and John the brother of James. And he cometh to the house of the ruler of the synagogue, and seeth the tumult, and them that wept and wailed greatly. And when he was come in, he saith unto them, Why make ye this ado, and weep? the damsel is not dead, but sleepeth. And they laughed him to scorn. But when he had put them all out, he taketh the father and the mother of the damsel, and them that were with him, and entereth in where the damsel was lying. And he took the damsel by the hand, and said unto her, Talitha cumi; which is, being interpreted, Damsel, I say unto thee, arise. And straightway the damsel arose, and walked; for she was of the age of twelve years. And they were astonished with a great astonishment (Mark 5:35-42, KJV).

A desperate man, a pressing request, bad news from home, shrieks of naysayers, and the laughter of mockery are the factors our Lord avails Himself of in order to teach us how to resist the resolution of the mockers and to press ahead undaunted. With high courage and daring faith, our Lord raised the 12-year-old daughter of Jairus from the dead. However, before the miracle could be made manifest, He had to ignore and distance Himself from those who "laughed him to scorn." This is the great key to victory. Mockers can be and ought to be ignored. Mark tells us that Jesus "put them all out." The time would come in His life when He would be unable physically to remove them, but He continued to ignore them.

> And when they had platted a crown of thorns, they put it upon his head, and a reed in his right hand: and they bowed the knee before him, and mocked him, saying, Hail, King of the Jews! And they spit upon him, and took the reed, and smote him on the head. And after that thy had mocked him, they took the robe off from him, and put his own raiment on him, and led him away to crucify him. And as they came out, they found a man of Cyrene, Simon by name: him they compelled to bear his cross. And when they were come unto a place called Golgotha, that is to say, a place of a skull, They gave him vinegar to drink mingled with gall: and when he had tasted thereof, he would not drink. And they crucified him, and parted his garments, casting lots: that it might be fulfilled which was spoken by the prophet, They parted my garments among them, and upon my vesture did they cast lots. And sitting down they watched him there (Matt. 27:29-36, KJV).

In the home of Jairus and along the bloody path to Calvary, Jesus turned a deaf ear to the mocking voices that clamorously challenged His godliness. If you focus on your mission and your Maker, you can't think about your mockers or what they say or do. During the days of our Lord, there were professional mourners. In ancient Palestine, these professional mourners were hired by the dead person's family to shed tears over the body. On the day of death, the deceased body was carried through the streets, followed by mourners, family members, and sympathetic friends and neighbors. When Jesus spoke of the girl being asleep and not dead, the professional mourners may have felt that their payment was in jeopardy and, therefore, laughed scornfully to chase away the threat. It is also conceivable that the mockers were people with lean faith and saw death as final. Regardless of the motive, our Lord set His course for a miracle and resisted all attempts to dissuade Him. By doing so, He left the mockers out of bounds to carry on with their foolishness. This world is on the prowl for people with the personal magnetism to stay their God-given course. Be one of them. Somebody is waiting to be raised. Somebody is desperate for a helping hand that doesn't want a hand out. Our Lord impacted history because He knew how to keep going in spite of global mockery. The background against which He worked was a dramatic power struggle, and yet, it was written by an unknown author, "I am far within the mark when I say that all the armies that ever marched, and all the navies that were ever built, and all the parliaments that ever sat and all the kings that ever reigned, put together, have not affected the life of man upon the earth as powerfully as has this one solitary life."

3. The mockers want to dethrone you. Don't encourage them.

And the LORD visited Sarah as he had said, and the LORD did unto Sarah as he had spoken. For Sarah conceived, and bare Abraham a son in his old age, at the set time of which God had spoken to him. And Abraham called the name of his son that was born unto him, whom Sarah bare to him, Isaac. And Abraham circumcised his son Isaac being eight days old, as God had commanded him. And Abraham was an hundred years old, when his son Isaac was born unto him. And Sarah said, God hath made me to laugh, so that all that hear will laugh with me. And she said, Who would have said unto Abraham, that Sarah should have given children suck? for I have born him a son in his old age. And the child grew, and was weaned: and Abraham made a great feast the same day that Isaac was weaned. And Sarah saw the son of Hagar the Egyptian, which she had born unto Abraham, mocking. Wherefore she said unto Abraham, Cast out this bondwoman and her son: for the son of this bondwoman shall not be heir with my son, even with Isaac. And the thing was very grievous in Abraham's sight because of his son. And God said unto Abraham, Let it not be grievous in thy sight because of the lad, and because of thy bondwoman; in all that Sarah hath said unto thee, hearken unto her voice; for in Isaac shall thy seed be called (Gen. 21:1-12, KJV).

The mockery by Ishmael of Isaac resulted in Ishmael's demise and departure from the household of Abraham. Isaac was the son of promise, and no mockery by Ishmael could nullify that divine right. The Bible is silent concerning Isaac's response to Ishmael's gesture. That silence, in and of itself, may be powerfully instructive. Could it be that the Bible is silent because Isaac bore the mockery in silence? Might it be that the Bible says nothing relating to Isaac's response because nothing is exactly what Isaac did? Is it not possible that Isaac was so secure in his position that he pronounced the mockery of Ishmael as a trivial annoyance, too unworthy and uneventful to warrant a response? Isaac's birth secured his seat, and your "second birth" secures your entry into a royal household. The blood of Jesus guarantees your birthright. You are now a son (prince) or a daughter (princess) of the King. Your enemies want to dethrone you, but they can't. They will use mockery to minimize your royal standing; hence, the temptation. One can be a prince and live like a pauper; one can be a princess and turn her back upon her royal station and languish away in a foreign country at the social base of that societal structure. Don't do it. Just because you are a prince or princess does not mean that you will be famous. God has not called you to be famous. God calls you to be faithful. Mockers attack your fame potential. Let them do so without your agony as you deal with it as if it is unobtrusive.

The state of Tennessee is the 16th state of the union. It has earned the nickname as the Volunteer State. This happened during the 1800s when America was involved in the wars of expansion. Tennessee natives volunteered in massive numbers during the War of 1812 and the Mexican War. The state became nationally known as a state where large numbers of people would volunteer and go to war for the issues and matters that were important to them. Famous volunteers like Davy Crockett and Sam Houston did not earn the state its nickname. It was the fact that there were thousands of unknowns who sacrificed without notoriety or fame, which moved the rest of the states to label Tennessee as the Volunteer State. God knows your name. He surveys your deeds, and He positions you in the Kingdom to reign.

One day, King Solomon observed a strange set of circumstances, and he documented it in the Book of Ecclesiastes. He wrote,

> There is an evil which I have seen under the sun, as an error which proceedeth from the ruler: Folly is set in great dignity, and the rich sit in low place. I have seen servants upon horses, and princes walking as servants upon the earth. (Eccl. 10:5-7, KJV).

Instead of riding, royalty was walking while servants assumed their riding positions. Something happened. Sovereigns walked and servants rode in a total reversal of roles. The apostle Paul brings the matter of dominion under New Testament scrutiny. God's amazing grace has redeemed humankind through the death of the Lord, Jesus Christ. "For if by one man's offense death reigned by one; much more they which receive abundance of grace and the gift of righteousness shall reign in life by one, Jesus Christ" (Rom. 5:17, KJV). Those who have received God's gift of grace and righteousness in Jesus Christ are to "reign in life."

The Bible does not define Christians as doormats waiting to be walked on. We are secure in our roles as servants of our Lord because we are fastened in our relationships as sons and daughters of the King. Our justification makes a blessed insight that keeps turbulence from interrupting our peace and grief from sapping our joy. Children of God, you have a horse to ride. Don't encourage your enemies by living beneath your blessed privileges. While Isaac may have remained silent in the face of Ishmael's mockery, his mother, Sarah, didn't. Sarah intervened, and Ishmael was cast out. The lesson is too obvious for argument. If you give God a chance, He can speak to your mockers through far more effective lips than your own. Lay claim to the promises of your Father, whose atmosphere of power will be born wherever your lot is cast.

CHAPTER VI

Your Enemies Don't Know Who They Are Not

And this is the record of John, when the Jews sent priests and Levites from Jerusalem to ask him, Who art thou? And he confessed, and denied not; but confessed, I am not the Christ. And they asked him, What then? Art thou Elias? And he saith, I am not. Art thou that prophet? And he answered, No. Then said they unto him, Who art thou? that we may give an answer to them that sent us. What sayest thou of thyself? He said, I am the voice of one crying in the wilderness, Make straight the way of the LORD, as said the prophet Esaias (John 1:19-23, KJV).

John the Baptist never tried to play Messiah because he knew who he was not. The seeds of prophecy had been faithfully sown and watered by undying intercession, and John was the closest thing that the masses could define as the answer to four hundred years' worth of prayers. Direct and confrontational, he did not merit membership in the local ministerial fellowship and religious hierarchy, but masses flocked to hear him. Bold and brilliant, he lit a fire where masses felt fires could no longer burn. He denounced evil and took God at His word, and crowds flocked to see him from sunrise to sunset. John's impact was so great that some mentioned him as a shoe-in candidate for the unfilled seat of the Messiah, but he said, "I am not." Regardless of overflowing crowds and beguiling compliments stored up in questions concerning his identity, John refused to think of himself in any role other than his own. When asked, he answered, "I am not the Christ" before he acknowledged, "I am the voice."

Benjamin Franklin once said, "If you would not be forgotten as soon as you are dead and rotten, either write things worth the reading or do things worth the writing." If you will "do things worth the writing," you will do them in spite of the words and works of enemies who don't know who they are not. Your enemies will appraise your worth because they don't know that they can't determine your value. Your enemies will judge you harshly because they don't know that they are not your judges. Veiled in the prophecies of doom, your enemies' verbalizations concerning your well-being and your future reveal dramatic ignorance of both their identity and ability. In spite of their most energetic efforts, your enemies aren't your determining factors for either success or failure. Asaph insightfully records,

> I said unto the fools, Deal not foolishly: and to the wicked, Lift not up the horn: Lift not up your horn on high: speak not with a stiff neck. For promotion cometh neither from the east, nor from the west, nor from the south. But God is the judge: he putteth down one, and setteth up another (Ps. 75:4-7, KJV).

With abiding conviction, Daniel witnessed before a troubled Babylonian king, declaring, "Blessed be the name of God for ever and ever: for wisdom and might are his: And he changeth the times and the seasons: he removeth kings, and setteth up kings: he giveth wisdom unto the wise, and knowledge to them that know understanding" (Dan. 2:20-21, KJV). Regardless of where you are—in prison, Paris, or Pennsylvania—"wisdom and might are [God's]."

After God delivered the promised son to Hannah, she made her way back into the house of the Lord in Shiloh and prayed:

> There is none holy as the LORD: for there is none beside thee: neither is there any rock like our God. Talk no more so exceeding proudly; let not arrogancy come out of your mouth: for the LORD is a God of knowledge, and by him actions are weighed. The bows of the mighty men are broken, and they that stumbled are girded with strength. They that were full have hired out themselves for bread; and they that were hungry ceased: so that the barren hath born seven; and she that hath many children is waxed feeble. The LORD killeth, and maketh alive: he

bringeth down to the grave, and bringeth up. The Lord maketh poor, and maketh rich: he bringeth low, and lifteth up. He raiseth up the poor out of the dust, and lifteth up the beggar from the dunghill, to set them among princes, and to make them inherit the throne of glory: for the pillars of the earth are the LORD's, and he hath set the world upon them. He will keep the feet of his saints, and the wicked shall be silent in darkness; for by strength shall no man prevail. The adversaries of the LORD shall be broken to pieces; out of heaven shall he thunder upon them: the LORD shall judge the ends of the earth; and he shall give strength unto his king, and exalt the horn of his anointed (1 Sam. 2:2-10, KJV).

A. By Strength Shall No Man Prevail

In the spirit of both prayer and prophecy, Hannah declared, "For by strength shall no man prevail;" she was right. It doesn't matter if your enemies define themselves as "up and in" while they scornfully view you as "down and out." The Bible affirms, "For by strength shall no man prevail." Oftentimes, your enemies will work feverishly while their contempt for you rises as you go from victory to victory. They know precisely what the outcome ought to be, but what they don't know is that written into the very constitution of the universe is the eternal, unchanging decree that proclaims, "By strength shall no man prevail." Hannah declared, "He will keep the feet of his saints." Saved, secure, selected, and sanctified, we are God's own, and everything that belongs to Him is under His protection, which includes our very feet, "the lowest portion of [the] body." We all know He'll keep our heads, hands, and hearts, but some don't know that God is committed to keeping our feet, as well. And, when God keeps our feet, He secures solid ground upon which we can stand that never shakes, in spite of the worst of the worst earthquakes. Even when others shall be swept away in a mighty outpouring of nature's wrath, God has promised to keep the feet of His own. Fearful convulsions and shaken cities might sweep away fortunes, forests, and fine dwellings, but God is committed to keeping the feet of His saints.

78

> The steps of a good man are ordered by the LORD: and he delighteth in his way. Though he fall, he shall not be utterly cast down: for the LORD upholdeth him with his hand (Ps. 37:23-24, KJV).

If ever there were a case where strength should have prevailed, it was in the epic battle of Goliath the warrior verses David the shepherd in 1 Samuel, chapter 17. Standing more than nine feet tall, wearing a bronze helmet and shin guards, Goliath wore body armor that weighed about one hundred twenty-five pounds. He carried a spear two inches thick that had an iron head that weighed close to fifteen pounds.

> And the Philistine drew near morning and evening, and presented himself forty days (1 Sam. 17:16, KJV).

Some giant-size problems, like a nagging head cold, have a way of hanging around in spite of our best home remedies, best wishes, and best prayers. There are some problems you can't wish or pray away...you have to face them and fight them. It could be Enron, City Hall, disease, doubt, depression, debt, and/or disgrace. Remember that the Book of 1 Samuel was not written before David defeated Goliath. Sometimes, in His wisdom, God selects us to be the first fresh witness for our unique age. Sometimes, God is writing a new story and casting us in starring roles to bless unborn generations. You could be God's new Esther, coming "to the kingdom for such a time as this" (Est. 4:14), or you just might be God's latter-day David, commissioned to confront "in the name of the LORD of hosts, the God of the armies of Israel" (1 Sam. 17:45, KJV).

B. Outsized Is Not Outmatched

Goliath was a giant. David was a youth. But God knows how to make a perfect match. David didn't go to the gym, and Goliath's muscles didn't turn to body fat. God created the earth to rotate on its axis at about one thousand miles an hour. If it rotated more quickly, the earth would burn up, and if it rotated more slowly, it would freeze up. God's work is always a perfect work. God tilts the earth perfectly. The earth is tilted at an angle of 23 degrees, and it gives us four seasons. If it were not tilted, the North and South Poles would be in eternal twilight. The water vapor would move north and south. The continents would pile up with ice and leave between themselves vast deserts. If the tilt were not correct, oceans would be lowered, and rainfall on all parts of the earth would be diminished, with horrible consequences. If the crust of the earth were ten feet thicker, there would be no oxygen, and plant and animal life could not survive. If the atmosphere were thinner, meteors that now burn out in the atmosphere would strike the earth by the millions each day. Traveling from six to forty miles a second, these fiery meteors would set fire to everything combustible on the earth. God's work is always a perfect work.

God regulates the tides with perfection. If all the air of the earth were liquefied, the earth would be covered with more than thirty feet of water. The moon is located 240 thousand miles away, and twice daily, the tides rise and fall because of the moon. If the moon were closer, the tides would be too vast and destroy twice per day all of the lowlands of the earth. If the continents were then washed away, the average depth of water over the earth would be one and one-half miles, and life could not exist. God knows how to strike the right balance. Believing in God's ability to balance, to match, and to empower, David arrived on the battlefield, confronted the giant, and defeated him. He, however, had to do it in spite of taunting from two sources who didn't know who they were not. Your enemies are not experts on your abilities. Don't treat their advice as if they are.

By the time David arrived on the battlefront, Goliath had crossed the ravine at the base of the valley and was strolling arrogantly on the side where the army of Israel had cast its tents. David was not sent to the battlefield to fight. His father, Jesse, had sent him on an errand to deliver roasted grain and cuts of cheese to his older brothers. It really doesn't matter how you get to your hour of victory. What matters is that you claim it regardless of any and all efforts to unnerve you. Giants are aggressive. They can be intimidating in and of themselves. When you have the partnership of giant aggression plus dampening verbosity, thoughts that routinely are centered on God get displaced. "Thou wilt keep him in perfect peace, whose mind is stayed on thee: because he trusteth in thee" (Isa. 26:3, KJV). David's older brother attacked David with an unkind assessment, saying, "I know thy pride, and the naughtiness of thine heart; for thou art come down that thou mightest see the battle" (1 Sam. 17:28, KJV). David responded, "What have I now done? Is there not a cause? And he turned from him toward another, and spake after the same manner; and the people answered him again after the former manner. And when the words were heard which David spake, they rehearsed them before Saul: and he sent for him" (1 Sam. 17:29-31, KJV).

Take special notice of verse 30, "And he turned from him toward another." Now, look carefully at verse 31, "And when the words were heard…they rehearsed them before Saul: and he sent for him." David didn't burn himself out on his brother, Eliab. He spoke about the giant, "and he turned from him toward another." Just as Eliab didn't know what was in David's heart, neither can your enemies read yours. Just as Eliab had no reluctance in speaking a mean appraisal concerning David, neither will your enemies demonstrate any apprehension in mislabeling your motives and abilities. Speak what you must, and, like David, turn from them to another. David kept his mind on Goliath, and you must keep your focus on your giant because your giant is your pathway to victory.

David's words would never have reached the ears of King Saul if he had not turned from Eliab to another. Your enemies don't know what is going on between you and God. There comes a time in this life when only you and God know what is going on between the two of you. There are certain pivotal moments when not even friends or family can discern the victory that will result from your trials.

A small boy looked at the picture of his absent father and said to his mother, "I wish my Daddy would just step out of that picture." God has made this world as a picture of Himself. Neither the sands beneath our feet nor the stars above our heads reveal His heart, but at Bethlehem, God stepped out of the picture. Stars look great, but they can't love us. Flowers are beautiful, but they have no hearts. Flowers will go to a wedding and to a funeral and never know the difference between the two events. But the God of creation is in Jesus. The God of redemption personally equips, visits, and works in us, in spite of what others think, hope, or say. Because the God who made the mountains that rest their rock-ribbed brows on the bosom of floating clouds has personally stepped out of the picture into individual lives, no enemies have the final say. Your enemies don't know what you can do. When they speak, like David, turn from them toward another. They don't know that they don't know what is going on between you and God.

The more determined David became to fight Goliath, the more forceful others spoke in their attempts to dishearten him. Eliab not only spewed out a torrent of resentment, but King Saul chimed in, saying, "Thou art not able to go against this Philistine to fight with him: for thou are but a youth, and he a man of war from his youth" (1 Sam. 17:33, KJV). Hockey star Wayne Gretzky and basketball superstar Michael Jordan have both been quoted as saying, "You miss one hundred percent of the shots you never take." The skeptics and prophets of doom will be drawn to you as bees are to honey when you reach your pathway to victory. When your enemies voice their predictions of failure, they are simply voicing their hopes rather than your chances. Your enemies don't want to see you try. They will rip the champion out of you if you give them the permission to do so. The good news for you is that, just as enemies are watching for a chance to deflate your hopes, God is waiting for a chance to equip you with a courage that will not run, a faith that will not doubt, a confidence that will not betray, a boldness that will not falter, and an honor that will not retreat. How God does what He does in us and through us is both a miracle and a mystery. I can't fully understand how God gives us victories over our enemies. David didn't understand it either, but being no stranger to danger, he said to Saul, "Thy servant kept his father's sheep, and there came a lion, and a bear, and took a lamb out of the flock: And I went out after him, and smote him, and delivered it out of his mouth: and when he arose against me, I caught him by his beard, and smote him, and slew him. Thy servant slew both the lion and the bear" (1 Sam. 17:34-36, KJV). David simply recalled his history with God in the face of danger. He didn't try to explain it. Such will be your experience as you mature in your walk with God.

I can't understand how it is that tears of joy and tears of sorrow flow from the same eye ducts, without any chemical differences in their makeup, but they do. I don't understand how it is that a sheep and a pig can graze in the same alfalfa fields, and for the sheep, it produces wool, and for the pig, it produces hair, but it does. I don't understand how an ant knows the difference between salt and sugar before tasting either, but it does. I don't understand how birds learn their songs without a teacher and never have rehearsals. I don't understand how mockingbirds can copy the musical notes of other birds without practice, but they do. I don't understand how spiders weave their webs without a pattern or how bees manufacture their honey to the taste of both beast and men, but they do. The spider has no loom, and the bee has no recipe detailing the exact sweetness of the honey, but both the spider and the bee get their jobs done. So it is with God; He gets the job done. I can't explain it, but my soul knows that it is so. As Goliath drew closer to David, he inched closer to death. David's slingshot and stone got the job done because of God's power. It wasn't skill; it was God. David triumphantly stood over the defeated giant and cut off the giant's head with his own huge sword. Whatever giant you face, remember, it is not as big as the power of God. "Now know I that the Lord saveth his anointed: he will hear him from his holy heaven with the saving strength of his right hand. Some trust in chariots, and some in horses: but we will remember the name of the Lord our God. They are brought down and fallen: but we are risen, and stand upright" (Ps. 20:6-8, KJV). With God's help, David defeated a lion, a bear, and Goliath. With that same available help, you can too, regardless of what your enemies say, do, or hope.

Your enemies are not the voices that give validity to your prophecies.

> Then Elisha said, Hear ye the word of the LORD; Thus saith the LORD, Tomorrow about this time shall a measure of fine flour be sold for a shekel, and two measures of barley for a shekel, in the gate of Samaria. Then a lord on whose hand the king leaned answered the man of God, and said, Behold, if the LORD would make windows in heaven, might this thing be? And he said, Behold, thou shalt see it with thine eyes, but shalt not eat thereof…. And the people went out, and spoiled the tents of the Syrians. So a measure of fine flour was sold for a shekel, and two measures of barley for a shekel, according to the word of the LORD. And the king appointed the lord on whose hand he leaned to have the charge of the gate: and the people trode upon him in the gate, and he died, as the man of God had said, who spake when the king came down to him. And it came to pass as the man of God had spoken to the king, saying, Two measures of barley for a shekel, and a measure of fine flour for a shekel, shall be tomorrow about this time in the gate of Samaria: And that the lord answered the man of God, and said,

Now, behold, if the LORD should make windows in heaven, might such a thing be? And he said, Behold, thou shalt see it with thine eyes, but shalt not eat thereof. And so it fell out unto him: for the people trode upon him in the gate, and he died (2 Kings 7:1-2, 16-20, KJV).

In your walk with Him, from time to time, God will lay an incredible prophetic word on your heart and lips concerning your future. Regardless of their dogmatic negativity, your enemies don't know "jack" about what's going to happen tomorrow. Fashioned for faith and not fear, you must, at times, become the voice that gives hope for tomorrow. We are inwardly constructed by God in nerve tissue, brain cell, and soul to walk by faith and not by sight. The human need for faith is not something imposed on us dogmatically but is something written in us intrinsically by our Maker. Christians are built for prophecy because they are built for faith.

In the city of Samaria, during the market days of the prophet Elisha, five quarts of flour cost a half an ounce of silver, and 10 quarts of barley grain cost only half an ounce of silver as well. This was the marketable price of those goods prior to a siege of the city by King Benhadad of Syria. The city, caught off guard, was reduced to a sad and sorrowful scene, caught in the grips of terrible want. Food was so scarce that a donkey's head sold for as much as two pounds of silver, and even a cup of dove's waste commanded the price of about two ounces of silver. With all food supplies gone, the famine progressed to such a state of severity that some mothers resorted to cannibalism (see 2 Kings 6:24-30). With this depressing circumstance serving as the backdrop of tragedy, Elisha spoke an incredible word of prophecy. He said, in essence, "By tomorrow, the city will be so stocked with food that foodstuffs will return to their normal prices." Unwilling to hear, heed, or believe, a courtier whom the king favored greatly said it could not happen. He went on to speculate that even if God opened the windows of heaven and poured down corn, the fulfillment of Elisha's prophecy would still go unfulfilled. Knowing that the king's courtier's validation was not necessary for God to bring the matter to pass, Elisha informed him of the cost of his unbelief. Elisha said, "You will see it happen, but you won't eat a single bite."

God went to work. He took four lepers, a deluge of speeding chariots and moving horses, some fear in the army of Aram, and some benevolence from outcasts and brought the prophecy to fruition. The man who doubted the prophecy lived to see God's deliverance of the city. The king appointed the officer to regulate traffic at a gate of the city, where he was trampled to death as a result of the rush of people. You don't need your enemies' validation of your God-given prophecies. They can't see into God's will for your future with any greater accuracy than the courtier who balked at Elisha's prophecy or the men who said the Titanic was unsinkable.

On the night of April 14, 1912, at 11:40 p.m., the great Titanic ship, the pride of the White Star fleet, ran into an iceberg approximately eight hundred miles from the coast of Newfoundland and sank. According to Senate inquiry reports, there were 2,223 people on board; 706 were saved, and 1,517 people drowned. The designers, owners, builders, crew, and passengers had all believed that the Titanic was an unsinkable ship. It was, at that time, the largest vessel ever to sail the waters. It was 882½ feet long. The anchors weighed 15½ tons, with each chain link weighing 175 pounds. It had a double bottom that was five to six feet thick. There were 15 watertight compartments. The crew didn't even take enough lifeboats because they thought the Titanic was unsinkable. The Titanic only had 20 lifeboats. Most lifeboats had the capacity to carry 65 people. Of the 2,223 people on the ship, only 1,176 of them could have been saved if each life boat had been filled to capacity. Crew members had not been assigned to man the boats until after the ship had sailed, and no drills had been run. Some boats had no water, sails, or compasses. Many of the people who went down with the ship could have survived if they had only gotten into the lifeboats, but few did. Lifeboats pulled away from the doomed ship with only ten to fifteen people, when most had the capacity to carry 65. There was plenty of room in many of the lifeboats, but until the end, many people didn't believe that the Titanic would sink.

There was another ship only ten miles away from the sinking Titanic. The captain of that vessel later told a senatorial committee investigating the disaster, "I didn't realize that the Titanic was sinking." When questioned about why his crew didn't hear the calls for help, the captain said that they had turned off their communication devices. When asked why they didn't see the Titanic sinking, the captain said, "We didn't know it was sinking because, you see, as deck by deck went down below the waters, and the lights went out one by one, we thought the ship, being faster than we, sailed off into the night." The Titanic sank as a result of hitting an iceberg. Some didn't believe that there were icebergs in the waters, and others didn't care. There were those who said the Titanic, with a gross registered tonnage of 46,328, traveling at 18 knots, could cut through any iceberg it hit. They were wrong, just as people are wrong when they think that your prophecies can't come true without their validation. The God of the Christian faith is the One who is able to do exceedingly above all that we ask or think.

It is said that "Joseph gathered corn as the sand of the sea, very much, until he left numbering; for it was without number" (Gen. 41:49, KJV). Afterwards, he became a ruler of Egypt, second only to Pharaoh. When the Queen of Sheba visited Solomon, she found that his wealth surpassed the rumors that had been floating; she remarked that the half had not been told (see 2 Chron. 9:6). Our God can do what we ask, above all we can ask, and exceedingly, abundantly above all we can ask. If we will keep alive in our memories the price God paid and the sacrifice our Lord made, we will be forever convinced of God's willingness to do exceedingly, abundantly above all we can ask (see Eph. 3:20).

There is, in an ancient city of Poland, a unique ceremony. It is more than seven hundred years old. For the past seven hundred years, at a designated time, a bugle has been sounded from the steeple of St. Mary's Church in Carcovia, Poland. The last note, I am told, is always discordant, sour, muffled, or out of tune. It sounds that way by design. The note is played in memory of a bugler who sounded the alarm one night as the city was being attacked by invading Tartars. Just as the bugler sounded the last notes of warning, he was shot in the chest by an arrow from the enemy and died at his post of duty while trying to save his people. He died in order that others might live. He died, but his sacrifice lived on from generation to generation. He died, but his fellows vowed never to forget his sacrifice. Each generation was reminded often that they didn't just show up but had climbed up on the back of one who died in order that they might live. When we consider the price our Father paid to redeem us by the precious blood of Jesus Christ, we should be convinced that He will abundantly do above anything we ask.

Your enemies are not the factors that affect your source of blessings.

> For if thou altogether holdest thy peace at this time, then shall there enlargement and deliverance arise to the Jews from another place; but thou and thy father's house shall be destroyed: and who knoweth whether thou art come to the kingdom for such a time as this? (Est. 4:14, KJV)

Your deliverance comes from the same source that sends your blessings. "Every good gift and every perfect gift is from above, and cometh down from the Father of lights, with whom is no variableness, neither shadow of turning" (James 1:17, KJV). Your enemies don't know the difference between a resource and a source, but you should. Your enemies might affect your resources. Your job, your supervisor, your friends, and your coworkers may all be resources. Some people take pride in their ability to deal you misery by turning people you may have counted on in the past against you. People, all people, are resources. God alone is our Source. Mordecai was so convinced that God was the source of all blessings and deliverance that he informed Queen Esther, "If thou altogether holdest thy peace at this time, then shall there enlargement and deliverance arise to the Jews from another place" (Est. 4:14, KJV). When friends turn away and foes turn up the pressure, God can send you enlargement and deliverance from another place. There is always another job, another friend, another resource, and another blessing.

Author John Whittier tells a wonderful story about a Christian Indian whose name was Nauhaught. Nauhaught had a dream one night in which he beheld an angel who dropped a gold piece into his hands. When Nauhaught awoke, he went out to monitor his traps but found nothing. His wife was sick, and his child was hungry, so he prayed and asked the Lord to send him the angel of his dream. Just as he concluded his prayer, he heard a clinking noise at his feet, and there on the ground, he found a purse full of gold coins. In his dream, the angel had given him only one coin. He wrestled with his conscience as he thought of his Christian responsibility. Suddenly, he saw a black snake coiled on the ground. He took the sight as a symbol of satanic temptation. He refused to take the purse as his own, saying, "I am deacon of the church, a baptized, praying Indian. If I did this thing, the trees, the birds, everything in nature would tell it. I would rather starve than steal." He hurried into town, stopped at the local inn, and inquired as to

whether anyone had lost anything. A husky sea captain identified the money. The captain decided to give 10 percent of
the recovered money to Nauhaught. He went home singing
praises to God. When the neighbors mentioned the skipper's
generosity, Nauhaught said to himself, "I saw an angel where
they see a man." Resources change, but God is the unchanging Source "with whom is no variableness, neither shadow of
turning" (James 1:17, KJV).

One of my favorite stories relates the experience of an
aged saint in dire need. The elderly lady prayed, asking the
Lord for some bread. Several mischievous boys heard her
supplications and decided to have some fun at her expense.
They put their money together, purchased several loaves of
bread, put the bread on the saint's doorstep, knocked on the
door, and hid in the shrubbery. The saint rejoiced as she
picked up the bag of bread with shouts of celebration, saying,
"Thank You, Jesus; thank You, Lord, and thank You, Father."
The boys sprang from behind the shrubs, laughing and saying, "Lady, we just pulled one over on you. God didn't send
you that bread. We did." The saint looked at them, and with
a million-dollar smile, said, "The devil might have brought it,
but it was the Lord who sent it." She was right. God sends,
even though He uses different resources to bring. Your enemies might rejoice when they stop the flow of one resource,
but "the earth is the Lord's, and the fullness thereof; the
world, and they that dwell therein" (Ps. 24:1, KJV).

God may, from time to time, prove to you that He is your
source by allowing you to deal with stressors. In the thirty-
second chapter of Genesis, verse 25, the Holy Spirit reveals
an insightful lesson on the subject: "And when he saw that he
prevailed not against him, he touched the hollow of his
thigh; and the hollow of Jacob's thigh was out of joint, as he
wrestled with him" (KJV). This record teaches us that God
loves to show us new dimensions of His glorious power. To
pacify Esau, Jacob offered 230 goats, 220 rams, 30 camels, 40

cows, 10 bulls, and 30 donkeys. Esau said no. The offering was not necessary. When God knocked Jacob's thigh out of joint, He was opening up the way for both a new name and a new dimension. Jacob had been a runner. Instead of increasing the runner's speed or strengthening his legs, God ended Jacob's sprinting career. Instead of giving Jacob a pair of Nike, Reebok, or K-Swiss shoes to help him run faster, God gave him a limp that would keep him from ever running again. And, of course, God had fixed Esau so that he kissed Jacob rather than kicking him. Sometimes, the Jacob in us has to be slain before the Israel in us can arise. When and if you get your limp from God, don't complain. It only means that you'll never need to run again.

CHAPTER VII

Your Enemies Don't Know that You Are Not in Their Hands but that They Could End Up in Your Debt

> And suddenly there was a great earthquake, so that the foundations of the prison were shaken: and immediately all the doors were opened, and every one's bands were loosed. And the keeper of the prison awaking out of his sleep, and seeing the prison doors open, he drew out his sword, and would have killed himself, supposing that the prisoners had been fled. But Paul cried with a loud voice, saying, Do thyself no harm: for we are all here. Then he called for a light, and sprang in, and came trembling, and fell down before Paul and Silas, And brought them out, and said, Sirs, what must I do to be saved? And they said, Believe on the Lord Jesus Christ, and thou shalt be saved, and thy house. And they spake unto him the word of the LORD, and to all that were in his house. And he took them the same hour of the night, and washed their stripes; and was baptized, he and all his, straightway (Acts 16:26-33, KJV).

The mighty really do fall. Great trees get uprooted and leave behind gaping spaces where they once stood proudly and punched holes in the sky. Authority can change hands, and seats of power can be unwillingly exchanged for defendant chairs and prison cells. Illusions of permanence sometimes dupe our enemies into believing they have everything fixed that ought to be fixed, every exit covered, and every escape hatch closed. However, with one swift and sweeping stroke, God can turn the tables, exchange roles, and demote those who are looking down with arrogance to those who are helplessly looking up for mercy. In a matter of hours, God exchanged the roles of the apostle Paul, the prisoner, and the unnamed Philippian jailer. The jailer had thrown the severely beaten apostles into the inner dungeon of the prison and locked their feet in chains. God, in His wisdom, takes this dreary scene and lights it as a candle of hope that will shine all over the world as goodness and righteousness are exchanged for evil and wickedness. When Paul and Silas prayed at midnight, God shook the jail with an earthquake. The jail doors flew open. The chains fell from the feet of all the prisoners. The trip between success and utter failure became short indeed. The journey from supervising to being supervised by those under his authority became so brief a journey that the jailer did not have time to consider the saga of changing roles and unforeseen events. Unsheathing his sword because he assumed that all of the prisoners had escaped, the jailer made the first gesture to take his own life rather than be executed for allowing a jailbreak. Paul saved his life, saying, "Do thyself no harm." Before the night gave way to the rising of the morning sun, the jailer and his whole house were saved. He, in deep debt to Paul, washed the men's wounds, fed them meat, and rejoiced in the salvation that his ex-prisoners had led him into as they crystallized God's plan of redemption with the words, "Believe on the Lord Jesus Christ, and thou shalt be saved." If Paul and Silas had remained in the hands of their enemies, the new day would have brought no stories of new life. If the jailer had been at the mercy of non-Christian men, his story would have ended in death rather than deliverance. Amazed at the swiftness of God's ability to change men's fortunes, David says in Psalm 37, verses 35-36,

> I have seen the wicked in great power, and spreading himself
> like a green bay tree. Yet he passed away, and, lo, he was not:
> yea, I sought him, but he could not be found (KJV).

God is a God of sovereign power, and He puts His sovereignty into action at will. Many times, God will show His hand by placing your enemy into your hands rather than out of your sight. Your enemies have little or no idea when they start a day that, before that day is over, they could fall deeply into your debt because God can decree that the only mercy they have access to is yours. God can ordain that your enemies' needs will be met according to your benevolence alone. The man on the Jericho road fell among thieves and was beaten up, passed up, and finally picked up by a certain Samaritan (Luke 10:30-36), and God can decree that your enemies be vulnerable to your good or ill will. Even when your enemies decide that you are the last person on earth they want to see looking down on them, God can mandate that you will be the only person they see on this earth. After your enemies have written you off, God can write you in and make you unavoidable. God can put you on the street where they have to walk and make your number the one they have to dial.

Elizabeth Elliot tells a wonderful story about a board that tilted against gravity. It is a story about her father as a small boy. One day, after climbing a ladder leaning against a house that was being built, he had a blessed and unique experience. He walked to the end of a board that was not securely nailed. The board slowly began to tip. He felt that he was doomed to a dangerous and maybe fatal fall, but inexplicably, the board righted itself as if a mighty hand had pushed it back into place. Her father could not explain the experience apart from believing that God's hand had intervened.

When I was only eight years old, my mother died suddenly. My father's love was a blessing beyond words, but the loss of a mother at that age is a sorrow that is almost beyond the ability of mortals to fully comprehend. As I walked from school during the first week of my life without my mother, my struggle was enlarged. Several older boys from my school began to throw rocks at me with deadly accuracy. They threatened me with promises of repeated aggression. I don't know why they chose to flesh out, at that time, their unprovoked aggression. I was alone, afraid, and afflicted. I didn't tell Daddy. I could see, even at that age, that he was struggling with his own sense of loss. I prayed and told God how afraid I was. I told Him how lonely I had been since He had taken my mother to live with Him. I poured out a child's deepest anguish. I went back to school the next day. That evening, as I walked home, the mean-spirited boys reappeared. However, a large, beautiful, snow-white dog was behind them. The dog chased the boys away. I reached out to touch it, but the dog remained beyond my reach as it escorted me home and then left me when I got close to my house. This mysterious dog spent a week with me as my escort. The boys who attacked me were so frightened by that dog that they became my protectors in order to win my favor. I have not seen that dog since that vulnerable week of my young life, but after almost fifty years, I remain convinced that God sent it. I cannot tell if it was angelic protection in the form of a dog or something else. I only know that it was an inexplicable act of God.

Saul in the debt of David

And it came to pass, when Saul was returned from following the Philistines, that it was told him, saying, Behold, David is in the wilderness of Engedi. Then Saul took three thousand chosen men out of all Israel, and went to seek David and his men upon the rocks of the wild goats. And he came to the sheepcotes by the way, where was a cave; and Saul went in to cover his feet: and David and his men remained in the sides of the cave. And the men of David said unto him, Behold the day of which the Lord said unto thee, Behold, I will deliver thine enemy into thine hand, that thou mayest do to him as it shall seem good unto thee. Then David arose, and cut off the skirt of Saul's robe privily. And it came to pass afterward, that David's heart smote him, because he had cut off Saul's skirt. And he said unto his men, The LORD forbid that I should do this thing unto my master, the LORD's anointed, to stretch forth mine hand against him, seeing he is the anointed of the LORD. So David stayed his servants with these words, and suffered them not to rise against Saul. But Saul rose up out of the cave, and went on his way. David also arose afterward, and went out of the cave, and cried after Saul, saying, My lord the king. And when Saul looked behind him, David stooped with his face to the earth, and bowed himself. And David said to Saul, Wherefore hearest thou men's words, saying, Behold, David seeketh thy hurt? Behold, this day thine eyes have seen how that the LORD had delivered thee today into mine hand in the cave: and some bade me kill thee: but mine eye spared thee; and I said, I will not put forth mine hand against my lord; for he is the LORD's anointed. Moreover, my father, see, yea, see the skirt of thy robe in my hand: for in that I cut off the skirt of thy robe, and killed thee not, know thou and see that there is neither evil nor transgression in mine hand, and I have not sinned against thee; yet thou huntest my soul to take it. The LORD judge between me and thee, and the LORD avenge me of thee: but mine hand shall not be upon thee. As saith the proverb of the ancients, Wickedness proceedeth from the wicked: but mine hand shall not be upon thee. After whom is the king of Israel come out? after whom dost thou pursue? after a dead dog, after a flea. The LORD therefore be judge, and judge between me and thee, and see, and plead my cause, and deliver me out of thine hand. And it came to pass, when David had made an end of speaking these words unto Saul, that Saul said, Is this thy voice, my son David? And Saul lifted up his voice, and wept. And he said to David, Thou art more right-eous than I: for thou hast rewarded me good, whereas I have rewarded thee evil. And thou has shown this day how that thou has dealt well with me: forasmuch as when the Lord had delivered me into thine hand, thou killedst me not. For if a man find his enemy, will he let him go well away? wherefore the LORD reward thee good for that thou has done unto me this day. And now, behold, I know well that thou shalt surely be king, and that the kingdom of Israel shall be established in thine hand. Swear now therefore unto me by the LORD, that thou wilt not cut off my seed after me, and that thou wilt not destroy my name out of my father's house. And David sware unto Saul. And Saul went home; but David and his men gat them up unto the hold (1 Sam. 24, KJV).

Saul in debt to David a second time

And the Ziphites came unto Saul to Gibeah, saying, Doth not David hide himself in the hill of Hachilah, which is before

Jeshimon? Then Saul arose, and went down to the wilderness of Ziph, having three thousand chosen men of Israel with him, to seek David in the wilderness of Ziph. And Saul pitched in the hill of Hachilah, which is before Jeshimon, by the way. But David abode in the wilderness, and he saw that Saul came after him into the wilderness. David therefore sent out spies, and understood that Saul was come in very deed. And David arose, and came to the place where Saul had pitched: and David beheld the place where Saul lay, and Abner the son of Ner, the captain of his host: and Saul lay in the trench, and the people pitched round about him. Then answered David and said to Ahimelech the Hittite, and to Abishai the son of Zeruiah, brother to Joab, saying, Who will go down with me to Saul to the camp? And Abishai said, I will go down with thee. So David and Abishai came to the people by night: and, behold, Saul lay sleeping within the trench, and his spear stuck in the ground at his bolster: but Abner and the people lay round about him. Then said Abishai to David, God hath delivered thine enemy into thine hand this day: now therefore let me smite him, I pray thee, with the spear even to the earth at once, and I will not smite him the second time. And David said to Abishai, Destroy him not: for who can stretch forth his hand against the LORD's anointed, and be guiltless? David said furthermore, As the LORD liveth, the Lord shall smite him; or his day shall come to die; or he shall descend into battle, and perish. The LORD forbid that I should stretch forth mine hand against the LORD's anointed: but, I pray thee, take thou now the spear that is at his bolster, and the cruse of water, and let us go. So David took the spear and the cruse of water from Saul's bolster; and they gat them away, and no man saw it, nor knew it, neither awaked: for they were all asleep; because a deep sleep from the LORD was fallen upon them. Then David went over to the other side, and stood on the top of an hill afar off; a great space being between them: And David cried to the people, and to Abner the son of Ner, saying, Answerest thou not, Abner? Then Abner answered and said, Who art thou that criest to the king? And David said to Abner, Art not thou a valiant man? and who is like to thee in Israel? wherefore then hast thou not kept thy lord the king? for there came one of the people in to destroy the king thy LORD. This thing is not good that thou has done. As the LORD liveth, ye are worthy to die, because ye have not kept your master, the LORD's anointed. And now see where the king's spear is, and the cruse of water that was at his bolster. And Saul knew David's voice, and said, Is this thy voice, my son David? And David said, It is my voice, my lord, O king. And he said, Wherefore doth my lord thus pursue after his servant? for what have I done? or what evil is in mine hand? Now therefore, I pray thee, let my lord the king hear the words of his servant. If the LORD have stirred thee up against me, let him accept an offering: but if they be the children of men, cursed be they before the LORD; for they have driven me out this day from abiding in the inheritance of the Lord, saying, Go, serve other gods. Now therefore, let not my blood fall to the earth before the face of the LORD: for the king of Israel is come out to seek a flea, as when one doth hunt a partridge in the mountains. Then said Saul, I have sinned: return, my son David: for I will no more do thee harm, because my soul was precious in thine eyes this day: behold, I have played the fool, and have erred exceedingly. And David answered and said, Behold the king's spear! and let one of the young men come over and fetch it. The LORD render to every man his righteousness and his faithfulness: for the LORD delivered thee into my hand today, but I would not stretch forth mine hand against the LORD's anointed. And, behold, as thy life was much set by this day in mine eyes, so let my life be much set by in the eyes of the LORD, and let him deliver me out of all tribulation. Then Saul said to David, Blessed be thou, my son David: thou shalt both do great things, and also shalt still prevail. So David went on his way, and Saul returned to his place (1 Sam. 26, KJV).

On two different occasions, Saul is vulnerable before the sword of David. In the stronghold of Engedi, Saul answered the "call of nature." There were caves everywhere in that bush highland of springs and waterfalls. Of all the caves Saul could have chosen to relieve himself, he walked directly into the one where David and his band of six hundred fighting men were hiding. Saul, sick with jealousy and paranoia, was unmercifully tracking David for the purpose of destroying him. Saul, caught in the grip of delusions with themes of jealousy and grandiosity, searched the land fiercely to destroy David. While his delusions may have been multiple, it is clear that they were organized around the theme of slaying

David. Having a superior and patronizing manner, Saul pursued his course without deviation. The ways of God are past finding out, and the issues common to this life often prove that unchanging reality. Saul had to go to the bathroom. He chose to do so in the privacy of a cave that could have become his coffin. Saul was exposed and at risk. David slipped up behind him, and instead of thrusting a spear in his back, he cut off a piece of his robe. Being a man after God's heart, David experienced justified guilt. Saul was far from what he should have been, but he was still God's anointed. David had humiliated Saul, and it troubled him because he knew what it meant to respect authority. How true is the statement, "A sensitive conscience is a great treasure and a valuable guide. Regardless of what you lose, don't lose your conscience." While clutching the piece of Saul's robe in his hand, David called out to Saul and informed him of the predicament from which he had arisen. Saul began to weep superficial tears out of a temporary conviction and said to David, "You are a better man than I am, for you have repaid me good for evil." Some people's tears mean little or nothing. Saul returned to his evil pursuit and plot to kill David. In the wilderness of Ziph, Saul was once again at the mercy of David. In His amazing grace and abiding mercy, God gave Saul a second chance to repay David for his kindness, but his heart had grown too hard. This time, Saul went to sleep with his spear next to him. David crept into the king's camp, and this time he took the king's spear and a cruse of water. Abishai, David's faithful nephew, urged David to kill Saul. The Bible here informs us that "[Saul and his army] were all asleep; because a deep sleep from the Lord was fallen upon them." Your enemies don't know that God can, at will, put them to sleep in your presence. I must, at this point, speak a direct word to you as a Christian. When God places your enemy before you in a helpless condition, He is also trying your faith. Pray for the grace not to strike your enemy when he/she is helpless. I know of no greater temptation than the temptation to act more like Saul than like the David that God has put in you. God's hand, not yours, is the hand that should strike the Sauls in your life. Resist the advice of the people in your life that are like Abishai. They may mean well, but they are not always wise.

Shimei in debt to David

Then said the king to Ziba, Behold, thine are all that pertained unto Mephibosheth. And Ziba said, I humbly beseech thee that I may find grace in thy sight, my lord, O king. And when king David came to Bahurim, behold, thence came out a man of the family of the house of Saul, whose name was Shimei, the son of Gera: he came forth, and cursed still as he came. And he cast stones at David, and at all the servants of king David: and all the people and all the mighty men were on his right hand and on his left. And thus said Shimei when he cursed, Come out, come out, thou bloody man, and thou man of Belial: The LORD hath returned upon thee all the blood of the house of Saul, in whose stead thou hast reigned; and the LORD hath delivered the kingdom into the hand of Absalom thy son; and, behold, thou art taken in thy mischief, because thou art a bloody man (2 Sam. 16:4-8, KJV).

And he bowed the heart of all the men of Judah, even as the heart of one man; so that they sent this word unto the king, Return thou, and all thy servants. So the king returned, and came to Jordan. And Judah came to Gilgal, to go to meet the king, to conduct the king over Jordan. And Shimei the son of Gera, a Benjamite, which was of Bahurim, hasted and came down with the men of Judah to meet King David. And there were a thousand men of Benjamin with him, and Ziba the servant of the house of Saul, and his fifteen sons and his twenty servants with him; and they went over Jordan before the king. And there went over a ferry boat to carry over the king's household, and to do what he thought good. And Shimei the son of Gera fell down before the king, as he was come over Jordan. And said unto the king, Let not my lord impute iniquity unto me, neither do thou remember that which thy servant did perversely the day that my lord the king went out of Jerusalem, that the king should take it to his heart. For thy servant doth know that I have sinned: therefore, behold, I am come the first this day of all the house of Joseph to go down to meet my lord the king. But Abishai the son of Zeruiah answered and said, Shall not Shimei be put to death for this, because he cursed the Lord's anointed? And David said, What have I to do with you, ye sons of Zeruiah, that ye should this day be adversaries unto me? shall there any man be put to death this day in Israel? for do not I know that I am this day king over Israel? Therefore the king said unto Shimei, Thou shalt not die. And the king sware unto him (2 Sam. 19:14-23, KJV).

There is no script that God cannot flip. There is no change that needs to be made that God cannot make. If you will give God your case without giving Him a deadline, He will convince you that He can do anything but fail. If God tells you to go fishing for Moby Dick, the great white whale, with a Zebco 33 fishing reel and a 10-pound test line, go. But don't just go. Go ahead and buy yourself some cornmeal, hot sauce, tartar sauce, cooking oil, and sweet onions for your hush puppies, and get ready for a fish fry. Shimei assaulted David with verbal barbs and flying rocks. It was a down time; Absalom had risen up against him, and David had chosen to flee the city rather than fight and destroy his own son. Shimei milked David's fragile state, but it didn't take God long to change things. On David's way back to claim his rightful throne, Shimei ran up to him, begging for his forgiveness. David could have destroyed him but said no. Shimei was a villain, but at that point in time and place, David rose above vindictive behavior, and so can you. For hundreds of years, Western Europe held to a sincere belief that the world ended at the Pillars of Hercules. The Pillars of Hercules were two promontories at the eastern end of the Strait of Gibraltar. During the time of this belief system, the Spanish nation stamped coins with a depiction of the Pillars of Hercules, and underneath were the Latin words *ne plus ultra*, which meant "no more beyond." After explorers sailed through the Pillars and discovered the New World, Spain made a change on her coins. The Spanish coins still carried the Pillars of Hercules, but the inscription was changed to read *plus ultra*, which means "more beyond." The power of God is greater than any power in the universe. There is always more power than the power that you see. Just as God did not exhaust His power at creation, He does not deplete Himself of power in our redemption. The Red Sea, the Jordan River, and the walls of Jericho did not cause God to break a sweat. With Him, there is *plus ultra*; there is "more beyond."

By the power of the Cross, our faith in Christ initiates an eternal relationship with the God of "more beyond." "The just shall live by faith" (Rom. 1:17, KJV). When Pope Leo X authorized John Tetzel to grant indulgences for payment in order to build St. Peter's Cathedral, Martin Luther and others blasted the concept. They stood upon the solid foundation that sin could not be atoned for by way of money either in this world or beyond the grave. The Church, at that time, errantly taught that God would release one of the eternal punishment of sin in hell. It taught that punishment in hell or in a place called purgatory could be cancelled by prayer, penance, or almsgiving. There is a story that a man approached John Tetzel and informed him that he was going to commit a sin and wanted to know how much it would cost him if he paid to have his sin forgiven in advance. Tetzel, keen to make the most of the situation monetarily, set the price at $30. The man made the payment and robbed, of all people, John Tetzel. The thief took back his $30 plus all of the other money that the priest had upon his person. When he was finally caught and jailed, the man protested, claiming that he had already paid for the sin prior to committing it and, therefore, should not be held liable. Today, of course, we frown upon that kind of foolish thinking while, at the same time, we claim that the debt has been paid. Jesus paid it all. And yet, in His providence, God brings us into the debt of others and makes even the worst of our enemies indebted to us. He is truly the God of "more beyond." Your enemies don't know that, but you must never forget it. It will not only keep you from failing your tests but will also keep you from falling to pieces.

Saul of Tarsus in debt to Ananias

And Saul, yet breathing out threatenings and slaughter against the disciples of the LORD, went unto the high priest, And desired of him letters to Damascus to the synagogues, that if he found any of this way, whether they were men or women, he might bring them bound unto Jerusalem. And as he journeyed, he came near Damascus: and suddenly there shined round about him a light from heaven: And he fell to the earth, and heard a voice saying unto him, Saul, Saul, why persecutest thou me? And he said, Who art thou, LORD? And the LORD said, I am Jesus whom thou persecutest: it is hard for thee to kick against the pricks. And he trembling and astonished said, LORD, what wilt thou have me to do? And the LORD said unto him, Arise, and go into the city, and it shall be told thee what thou must do. And the men which journeyed with him stood speechless, hearing a voice, but seeing no man. And Saul arose from the earth; and when his eyes were opened, he saw no man: but they led him by the hand, and brought him into Damascus. And he was three days without sight, and neither did eat nor drink. And there was a certain disciple at Damascus, named Ananias; and to him said the LORD in a vision, Ananias. And he said, Behold, I am here, LORD. And the Lord said unto him, Arise, and go into the street which is called Straight, and inquire in the house of Judas for one called Saul, of Tarsus: for, behold, he prayeth, And hath seen in a vision a man named Ananias coming in, and putting his hand on him, that he might receive his sight. Then Ananias answered, LORD, I have heard by many of this man, how much evil he hath done to thy saints at Jerusalem: And here he hath authority from the chief priests to bind all that call on thy name. But the Lord said unto him, Go thy way: for he is a chosen vessel unto me, to bear my name before the Gentiles, and kings, and the children of Israel: For I will show him how great things he must suffer for my name's sake. And Ananias went his way, and entered into the house; and putting his hands on him said, Brother Saul, the Lord, even Jesus, that appeared unto thee in the way as thou camest, hath sent me, that thou mightest receive thy sight, and be filled with the Holy Ghost. And immediately there fell from his eyes as it had been scales: and he received sight forthwith, and arose, and was baptized (Acts 9:1-18, KJV).

Saul, according to the Bible, went forth, "breathing out threatenings and slaughter against the disciples of the Lord." The Greek word for slaughter is the word *phonos*. It means murder. Saul was determined to get rid of people like Ananias by means of murder. He didn't want only to hurt them. He desired to destroy them. As a representative of the powerful Sanhedrin council, Saul was determined to root out the Christian faith. The Sanhedrin wielded awesome power throughout the Jewish diaspora. The Roman Empire upheld their authority for more than one hundred years. Saul was a zealous man who was convinced that he was doing the will of God as he went forth to eradicate the work of the Son of God. Paul had secured written authority to extradite believers who were part of the diaspora and to deliver them to Jerusalem for trial, and Damascus became a high-value target. Determined to wreak violence upon believers and grounded by an insane, passionate resolve, Saul began his journey toward Damascus.

Charles Spurgeon once said, "Paul was a great man, and I have no doubt that on the way to Damascus he rode a very high horse. But a few seconds sufficed to alter the man. How soon God brought him down." On the road to Damascus, Saul suddenly found himself on the ground and without his sight. He saw a light, heard a voice, and found himself helpless in the presence of the almighty God. Thirty years after that humbling experience, Saul, who became Paul, wrote that Jesus had "apprehended" (Phil. 3:12, KJV) him on that same Damascus road. So it was that one moment, Saul of Tarsus

was secure in the impenetrable armor of his narrow preju-
dices, and the next moment, God had him lying prostrate on
the ground, blinded by a light to which this world could not
give birth.

Ananias, a man who had been the unnamed object of
Saul's aggression, quickly became the answer to his prayers.
Saul's reputation had preceded him. The whole city was both
buzzing and shaking with the news that the grand inquisitor
(Saul) was on the way to do the Sanhedrin's bidding.
Ananias was quickly removed from the category of potential
victim to that of a doorkeeper who led Paul into the fellowship of his new family. How true it is that God can change
things. How awesome it is that God can reverse roles and
make the last first and the first last. I have seen it time after
time, in place after place. God used Ananias' hands to
remove the scales from Paul's blinded eyes. It was Ananias'
voice that spoke the precious words, "Brother Saul," to a
helpless and defeated Saul. It was Ananias' prophecy that
gave Saul the knowledge that he was indeed a chosen vessel
in the kingdom of our Lord.

In the harbor of Syracuse, on the waterfront, there is a
statue of Archimedes, the great Greek engineer, who, at the
siege of Syracuse, set fire to the Roman Navy fleet by the
refraction of mirrors. It was Archimedes who said that if he
could find a place upon which to stand and rest his lever, he
could move the whole world. Two hundred years later, a ship
came sailing into the bay of Syracuse from Malta, and on that
ship was Saul, who became Paul. Even as a prisoner in chains
on his way to Rome to be beheaded, Paul had become the
man who had found a place upon which he could stand and
had found a mighty lever, in the Gospel, with which he was
moving the world. The charge raised against him at
Thessalonica was, "These [men] that have turned the world
upside down are come hither also" (Acts 17:6, KJV). How
amazing it is that the God who leads us in ways that startle

us can bring our enemies into our debt in order for some of them to find a place upon which to stand in order to move the world. God never forsakes you, even for a moment. The God who gives eyes to the blind and feet to the lame seems to take pleasure in bringing our enemies into our debt even as He makes them useful.

Unfailing constancy leads to unending conquests

> I know thy works, and tribulation, and poverty, (but thou art rich) and I know that blasphemy of them which say they are Jews, and are not, but are the synagogue of Satan. Fear none of those things which thou shalt suffer: behold, the devil shall cast some of you into prison, that ye may be tried; and ye shall have tribulation ten days: be thou faithful unto death, and I will give thee a crown of life (Rev. 2:9-10, KJV).

You are not in the hands of your enemies, even if they occupy seats of authority among or above you. Daily, we all bear witness to the fact that our world bears the scars of its sinful population. Redemption is not complete. It was the apostle Peter who wrote, "We, according to his promise, look for new heavens and a new earth, wherein dwelleth righteousness" (2 Pet. 3:13, KJV).

A small girl received a globe for Christmas. She was asleep one night when her parents went into her room to borrow the globe. As her mother lifted the globe from her nightstand, the child awakened and asked, "Mother, what are you doing with my world?" There are times when we wonder what is going on in our world. There are moments when hostile forces appear to exert far too much power over our world. When those times hit, there is a tendency in some to forget that our God can take care of us in all of our shifting circumstances and changing conditions. We must simply remain constant in our devotion and service, regardless of how strong our enemies appear to be.

If any people knew the perils of shifting circumstances, it was the church at Smyrna. If any people knew tribulations, it was those who made up this congregation of constancy. In spite of the boasts of enemies who perceived the church to be in their hands, the church at Smyrna was much like a steadfast ship on a stormy sea. Neither the relentless pressure of events nor the forces of circumstances had, in any manner, tattered her sails. Satan had secured a seat for himself in her midst, but the winds of chance and change had not diverted her from her course. With much difficulty, she was still plowing through the mad waters and making great progress toward port. While her lot had been one terrifying severe confrontation after another, her journey was above reproach. She had been constantly and consistently battered, but she was still in good form in regard to behavior, even while battling enemies, evil, and error. Smyrna had withstood the test of recurring slander. For her, such experiences built up self-confidence, self-control, self-development, and, on occasion, self-examination. This church had known a small pocket of dissension, but God kept her from going out of business. God made her pressure-proof. She had seen the humility of Jesus conquer pride, the love of Jesus conquer hate, the stripes of Jesus conquer sickness, the purity of Jesus conquer immorality, the peace of Jesus conquer hostility, and the Spirit of Jesus conquer the flesh. She was heavily endowed with spiritual graces. She was rich in faith, rich in grace, rich in good works, and rich in the Gospel. It has been said, "Skilled pilots gain their reputation from storms and tempests." And so often, it is our lot to persist when there is no tail wind and when the headwind is against us. As long as we are constant, God takes the responsibility. He steps in. In the midst of our exhausted possibilities, God establishes our going. If we will be people of conviction, we will be able to move the world. Daniel, as a man of conviction, caused kings to wait for his word. Nebuchadnezzar, Belshazzar, and Darius all waited upon Daniel because he had convictions. On the night when King Belshazzar was killed, a hand began to write upon the wall. The king saw it and was frightened. He promised Daniel honors and gifts. Daniel gave the king the correct interpretation and said, "Thou art weighed in the balances, and art found wanting" (Dan. 5:27, KJV). Daniel could have hedged a bit. He could have said he couldn't read the writing, but he didn't. He spoke the truth, and God kept and prospered him. Constancy leads to conquest.

John Wesley was a man of conviction. After he became established in the faith, all England and the world were moved. It is said, "John Wesley made the masses of England sin-conscious, God-conscious, and grace-conscious. He restored to them their souls. He opened their spiritual eyes and unstopped their spiritual ears." Another source declared, "Wesley brought forth water from the rocks to make a barren land live again." One gifted scholar said, "No man lived nearer to the center than John Wesley, neither Pitt nor Clive, neither Mansfield nor Johnson. You cannot cut him out of the national life. No single figure influenced so many minds. No single voice touched so many hearts. No other man did such a life's work for England." For 53 years following Wesley's great spiritual work, in the face of seemingly insurmountable odds, he fought and won. Many historians have agreed that Wesley saved England from the horrors of a French Revolution.

Whenever we give ourselves to God and stand as people of conviction, He finds a way to fill our hearts with a new and rapturous gladness. Even when our lives are difficult and the gates are many, the keys are never lost. Even when the roads are steep and the wind is bleak and the clouds are ominous, there is always a heavenly sound of music in the air. Even when the house is bare and silent and loved ones are out or gone, the Lord will cause us to hear His own coming and going in the stillness of the hour. In those moments when the tempter seeks to mislead and misinform, speak the following words: "The Lord God is my strength, and he will make my feet like hinds' feet, and he will make me to walk upon mine high places" (Hab. 3:19, KJV).

When thou passest through the waters, I will be with thee; and through the rivers, they shall not overflow thee: when thou walkest through the fire, thou shalt not be burned; neither shall the flame kindle upon thee (Isa. 43:2, KJV).

For the LORD shall be thy confidence, and shall keep thy foot from being taken (Prov. 3:26, KJV).

Jesus Christ's involvement with human beings is total and thorough. Our Lord is grounded in the soil of our roads and riveted to the the details of our lives. "He knows the pain you feel. He can save, and He can heal." Jesus is not standing at the end of some lonely road that you have to travel. He is with you, in the dust, in the dirt, in the debris, and even in the disasters, not simply cheering you along but strengthening you, step by step. When you make a resolution and link it with prayer, strength will be supplied to you step by step, job by job, test by test, and day by day.

There is a legend that has sparked both poetry and song. According to the legend, Joseph of Arimathea, who begged for our Lord's body and took it, with the help of Nicodemus, from the cross, carried a vessel. This unique cup was called the Holy Grail. According to legend, Joseph caught the blood that our Lord shed on the cross and carried it to Glastonbury, where you can still see the ruins of the cathedral on an island in Somerset. There, he formed the prestigious order of Royal Knights, whose duty it was to protect the blood. The head knight was made king. At certain seasons, the king unveiled the golden cup that held the precious blood. At that instant, a glorious and radiant light would fall on the faces of all the knights and endue them with strength from heaven. But, only the pure in heart could look upon that cup and behold the glorious light which streamed from the blood of Jesus. While this story has some beauty, I thank God that you don't have to be perfectly pure in heart in order to benefit from the blood of Jesus. The precious blood of Jesus Christ needs no protection from us, but it is able to be our protection in all circumstances. Your enemies have no knowledge of the power of the blood. If they did, they wouldn't be your enemies. They don't know that the blood of Jesus Christ cleansed us from all sin. Cleansed from sin, we are protected from all foes. "Behold, the Lord's hand is not shortened, that it cannot save; neither his ear heavy, that it cannot hear "(Isa. 59:1, KJV).

The promises of God touch every phase of life. Like the church at Smyrna, we can pass the tests of time and tide. The greatest condemnation of this greedy culture of ours is not that many are tainted with a false notion of success and smitten with a dangerous virus called materialism. That is bad and sad, but it is not the worst part of our culture. The worst part is that too many have communicated to their children that getting things is what matters most in this life. Your enemies can sometimes take things away from you. They can burn what can be burned. They can drown what can be drowned. But praise be to God that we are under the blood of Jesus, which cannot be burned, drowned, stolen, or lost. What we are, i.e. under the blood, helps burglars become believers and grants unsupervised access to a bank with unlimited funds. What we are, under the blood, makes us victorious in spite of cruel scrutiny. People look through both telescopes and microscopes, but the blood of Jesus protects us both close up and far off. Only the almighty God can cast one too far away to make a comeback. A past president of the National Baptist Convention was often heard saying, "If a man flings you, you can get up again. If a mule flings you, you might get up again. But, when God flings you, you are flung." High dreams and holy purposes were not blighted by the cross our Lord bore at Calvary. Neither will your high dreams be blighted, even if your enemies do their worst from seats of power. Constancy in devotion and service to God always places you within God's will. When you are living, working, and serving within God's will, you will know conquest. As you obey God, you get a chance to enjoy His fellowship. You are promised victory from He who lives victoriously. If ever there was a man who seemed to be defeated, it was Jesus as He made His way to Calvary. The great multitudes who had followed Him had turned away. Fondness had been traded for bitter hate and cold antagonism. His enemies' work had wrung from some sympathetic women bitter tears, and yet He looked at them and said, "Daughters of Jerusalem, weep not for me, but weep for yourselves, and for your children" (Luke 23:28, KJV). Why did Jesus say, "Weep not for me"? The answer is simple. He was in far better shape than He appeared to be. His enemies lifted Him up on a cross. But, that was not the end. Lifted up from the earth, He drew and still draws all men unto Himself—not some men but all men (see John 12:32). Some men will be drawn to Him as their Savior; others will be drawn to Him as their Judge; but one way or another, all men will be drawn to Him, the victorious Christ. He remains possessed of a quality that time cannot diminish and death cannot destroy. You are not in the hands of your enemies, but because the victorious Christ reigns, they might just end up in your debt.

CHAPTER VIII

Your Enemies Don't Know that They Have a Date to Do Duty in Dark and Slippery Places

> He disappointeth the devices of the crafty, so that their hands cannot perform their enterprise. He taketh the wise in their own craftiness: and the counsel of the froward is carried headlong. They meet with darkness in the day time, and grope in the noonday as in the night (Job 5:12-14, KJV).

A. Dark Places

There is something in the government of God, often unseen by men, that makes the wicked victims of their own traps. In spite of rapid speech and focused efforts to remove insinuations of blame, your enemies will, at some point, "meet with darkness in the day time, and grope in the noonday as in the night." As a matter of fact, God finds it humorous when wicked people plot. "The wicked plotteth against the just, and gnasheth upon him with his teeth. The LORD shall laugh at him: for he seeth that his day is coming" (Ps. 37:12-13, KJV). In scripture after scripture, we witness the poetry of God's justice at work in the world. In the Book of Esther, we see Haman being hanged upon the gallows he built for Mordecai. Jonah refused his first calling to preach to the people of Nineveh because he wanted to see them suffer, but it was he who experienced the "belly of hell" into which he wanted the people of Nineveh to fall. God has countless ways by which He can create darkness in daylight. When the Lord Jesus Christ was crucified at Calvary, there was a unique darkness that reigned from noon until three o'clock. People shook with fear. Some beat upon their breasts while others returned to their homes in stark terror. God created pitch blackness at noon. Neither the chief priests nor the scribes knew who they were dealing with when they had the Lord of life crucified. Both groups were too arrogant to realize that they were facing much more than a rambunctious bunch of radicals. They had aligned themselves against the almighty God, who is able to make any and all flesh and blood "meet with darkness in the daytime."

The Roman centurion charged with the assignment to crucify what seemed to be a peasant probably had seen many crucifixions prior to our Lord's, but he had never seen "darkness in the daytime." The earth began to quake, and rocks split. The "Rock of Ages" refused to break, but earthly rocks split as they paid homage to the Son of God. The veil of the Temple was ripped from top to bottom. If it had been torn from bottom to top, there could have been an earthly answer for the ripping. The ripping from top to bottom reveals the fact that the action came from above. Dirt began to fly through the air as if some force were shooting it from below the crust. Graves were opened, and the saints of the ages began to come out and walk the streets of Jerusalem.

In the Bible, darkness is not a good thing. God was not pleased when "darkness was upon the face of the deep" (Gen. 1:2, KJV). God separated the light from the darkness, and the psalmist says, "Thou makest darkness, and it is night: wherein all the beasts of the forest do creep forth" (Ps. 104:20, KJV). During the darkness of the night, the psalmist heard the roar of the lion. He imagined the night creatures emerging and the nocturnal animals creeping. During the darkness of night, colors lose their distinctiveness, and even the best of men and women stumble. Darkness brings about confusion, gloom, crudeness, and even a shadowy vulgarity. God knows what is in the darkness. "He revealeth the deep and secret things: he knoweth what is in the darkness, and the light dwelleth with him" (Dan. 2:22, KJV). "Yea, the darkness hideth not from thee; but the night shineth as the day: the darkness and the light are both alike to thee" (Ps. 139:12, KJV).

When Joshua recalled God's gracious dealings with Israel, he reminded them, "He put darkness between you and the Egyptians" (Josh. 24:7, KJV). One of the plagues that God sent upon Egypt was a plague of darkness (Exod. 10:21-23, KJV). Amon-Ra was the sun god of the Egyptians. He was also the chief god of all other Egyptian gods, but God sent darkness and covered the land of Egypt with it for three full days. Your enemies don't know that God can and will make their daylight into darkness, and there will be absolutely nothing they can do about it. It matters not if their plans are personal or local. God is able, and God is prone to defeat with darkness the best-laid evil plans that are built in the daytime.

Terrorists murdered Black Africans when they bombed Kenya's American Embassy; they shot a Blackhawk down in Somalia; they blew a hole in the side of an American warship and then unleashed massive terror on September 11, 2001. Their worldwide emphasis is seen via bombed trains in Spain, the Jihad terror manuals that propose the worldwide overthrow of all secular governments, and the people of Europe being troubled as Jihad-oriented clerics call for more deaths. These enemies can be defeated. We must, as a nation, reestablish a worldwide alliance against this worldwide threat, and we must, as Christians, pray that God will confront their evil as they look for light in their wicked and dark schemes. The Bible says, "Ye have not, because ye ask not" (James 4:2, KJV). It doesn't matter if your enemy is Osama bin Laden, Timothy McVeigh, Abu Nidal, John Doe, or your next door neighbor. God is able to assign darkness in the midst of daylight. Jeremiah knew this, and he spoke to his nation, saying, "Give glory to the Lord your God, before he cause darkness, and before your feet stumble upon the dark mountains, and, while ye look for light, he turn it into the shadow of death, and make it gross darkness" (Jer. 13:16, KJV).

1. Understand Who You Are in Christ

"So then faith cometh by hearing, and hearing by the word of God" (Rom. 10:17, KJV). You will never have the faith you need apart from knowledge of the Word of God. To pray for faith without hearing the Word of God is ineffective. God doesn't use shortcuts because He knows that faith is too important an asset to trivialize. Faith comes by hearing and hearing by the Word of God. In order to receive faith, you need knowledge of the Word of God. If you receive knowledge of God's Word, you will have faith. If you don't receive knowledge of God's Word, you will not have faith, and you will never have faith because "faith cometh by hearing and hearing by the Word of God." Your faith will grow as your understanding of the Word of God grows. The Bible teaches us that God can and will use darkness, but in Him, there is no darkness. "This then is the message which we have heard of him, and declare unto you, that God is light, and in him is no darkness at all" (1 John 1:5, KJV). God is light; therefore, darkness cannot exist in His presence. When God removes His holy presence to bless, darkness prevails. Christians live in His presence; therefore, as a Christian, you dwell "in the secret place of the most High" and "under the shadow of the Almighty" (Ps. 91:1, KJV). It is from this location in Christ that you can safely run the race set before you while your enemies are stumbling, blundering, floundering, lurching, and faltering in the darkness that comes during the daytime. As you grow in the knowledge of God's Word and dwell in Him, you will trade your fears for greater faith, thus overcoming easily what others cannot endure.

> Thou shalt not be afraid for the terror by night; nor for the arrow that flieth by day; Nor for the pestilence that walketh in

darkness; nor for the destruction that wasteth at noonday. A thousand shall fall at thy side, and ten thousand at thy right hand; but it shall not come nigh thee. Only with thine eyes shalt thou behold and see the reward of the wicked. Because thou hast made the LORD, which is my refuge, even the most High, thy habitation; There shall no evil befall thee, neither shall any plague come nigh thy dwelling. For he shall give his angels charge over thee, to keep thee in all thy ways. They shall bear thee up in their hands, lest thou dash thy foot against a stone. Thou shalt tread upon the lion and adder: the young lion and the dragon shalt thou trample under feet. Because he hath set his love upon me, therefore will I deliver him: I will set him on high, because he hath known my name. He shall call upon me, and I will answer him: I will be with him in trouble; I will deliver him, and honour him. With long life will I satisfy him, and show him my salvation (Ps. 91:5-16, KJV).

2. As Jesus Arose from the Grave, so Can You Rise Above the Darkness that Meets the Daytime.

And there came also Nicodemus, which at the first came to Jesus by night, and brought a mixture of myrrh and aloes, about an hundred pound weight. Then took they the body of Jesus, and wound it in linen clothes with the spices, as the manner of the Jews is to bury. Now in the place where he was crucified there was a garden: and in the garden a new sepulchre, wherein was never man yet laid. There laid they Jesus therefore because of the Jews' preparation day: for the sepulchre was nigh at hand (John 19:39-42, KJV).

The key to understanding the full power of our Lord's resurrection is found in the latter fragment of verse 40 of this nineteenth chapter of the Gospel of St. John. It says that they wound up the body of Jesus in linen according to the manner of the Jews regarding burial. Nicodemus brought a mixture of myrrh and aloes so great that John claimed it weighed about one hundred pounds. Stop and allow that factor to rattle your thinking as to the grave from which Jesus arose. Before the Lord confronted the sealed stone at the opening of the grave, He had to confront the hundred-pound mixture that encased His body. It was during their Egyptian captivity that the Jews learned the art of embalming from their captors. The Egyptians created a ropy, glue-like adhesive from myrrh and aloes. They then covered thin strips of cloth with the adhesive and wrapped the body in these strips of cloth. If you've seen pictures of ancient Egyptian mummies, you can get a visual of the goal of the process. This process made a sort of cocoon around the body. Each toe and finger was wrapped separately. One great motivating factor that sent the women to the tomb of Jesus "when it was yet dark" was the need to finish the embalming (John 20:1, KJV).

The face of the Lord had not been properly covered. The arrival of the Sabbath caught Nicodemus and Joseph of Arimathea before they could complete their work, so they left the face of Jesus open and laid a napkin over it. The glue-like adhesive hardened while the face of our Lord was covered with the napkin. When God raised Jesus from the dead, Jesus' entire body came out of the facial opening and left the hardened cocoon lying on the ground. He didn't fling the napkin to a corner but folded it neatly and prepared to greet the visitors that He knew would come. When the Disciples saw the cocoon lying unbroken and the napkin neatly folded, they knew that no human hands had carried the Lord away. No human hands could have done what had been done. No human hands could have expressed, revealed, disclosed, unveiled, or detailed that kind of glorious intervention. No human hands could have performed that indescribable, inconceivable, inexpressible, incomparable, unspeakable, unexplainable, and unperceivable event. This resurrection spoke and still speaks of a glory that transcends, exceeds, and excels all things that are visible or invisible.

The same power that raised our Lord from the grave will raise you above the darkness that meets the daytime. When you allow God's Word to woo you, you will find it to be "a lamp unto [your] feet, and a light unto [your] path"

(Ps. 119:105, KJV). The same power that infused every word Jesus said is available to "disappointeth the devices of the crafty" and send them groping "in the noonday as in the night." Your enemies don't know that they cannot keep you from being victorious, and they can't prevent a tour of duty for themselves in dark and slippery places.

> Now the God of peace, that brought again from the dead our Lord Jesus...through the blood of the everlasting covenant (Heb. 13:19-20, KJV).

The blood of Jesus does not refer only to His death but also to His life. Through the blood of Jesus, you are given a life that defies, strangles, and triumphs over death itself. The Bible tells us that death is the last enemy. By way of substitution and restitution, the blood of Jesus has relieved us from the judgment of God, which makes an eternal difference between you and your enemies. Your enemies think that you are their problem, but their problem comes as a result of the distinction that God makes between you and them because of the blood.

> And Moses said, Thus saith the LORD, About midnight will I go out into the midst of Egypt: And all the firstborn in the land of Egypt shall die, from the firstborn of Pharaoh that sitteth upon his throne, even unto the firstborn of the maidservant that is behind the mill; and all the firstborn of beasts. And there shall be a great cry throughout all the land of Egypt, such as there was none like it, nor shall be like it any more. But against any of the children of Israel shall not a dog move his tongue, against man or beast: that ye may know how that the LORD doth put a difference between the Egyptians and Israel (Exod. 11:4-7, KJV).

> And I, behold, I will harden the hearts of the Egyptians, and they shall follow them: and I will get me honour upon Pharaoh, and upon all his host, upon his chariots, and upon his horsemen. And the Egyptians shall know that I am the LORD, when I have gotten me honour upon Pharaoh, upon his chariots, and upon his horsemen. And the angel of God, which went before the camp of Israel, removed and went behind them; and the

pillar of the cloud went from before their face, and stood
behind them: And it came between the camp of the Egyptians
and the camp of Israel; and it was a cloud and darkness to
them, but it gave light by night to these: so that the one came
not near the other all the night (Exo. 14:17-20, KJV).

In Egypt, God made a difference between the Egyptians
and Israelites through the crimson blood of a Lamb. Before
the swift and swelling tides of the Red Sea, God made a difference through a cloud that came between them; it was a
cloud of darkness to the Egyptians, but it gave light by night
to God's people. If Pharaoh had stayed in Egypt, he would
never have witnessed the cloud that was "darkness to them."
If Israel had not obeyed God and exited Egypt, they never
would have experienced the cloud that gave them light in the
desert. According to Dr. Aaron Isaiah Jones of Gulfport,
Mississippi, there is a dangerous portion of water near a pier
where people at one time loved to swim. The perpetual danger of drowning lurked in a particular portion of deep and
dark water. The Gulfport natives called that water "the deadly drowning hole." A young man returned home from the
Navy after his tour of duty ended. He was an excellent swim-
mer and volunteered his time. Whenever someone unknow-
ingly swam past the place where the shallow water ended
and the deep step-off began, the young man would dive in
and rescue the would-be victim. He was not a paid lifeguard;
he did it because of two things: he could swim well, and he
loved people.

Similarly, Jesus Christ keeps an eternal vigil over His
own. He is the Master of the sea. Saving lives is His glorious
business. In the same city where there was weeping at the
death of the firstborn, God forbade even a dog to "move his
tongue" against His people.

In this life, there are many deadly drowning holes. Your
enemies don't know when they pass the place where the
shallow water ends and the dark, deep step-off begins, but

you do. Each time they attack you, they cross the line of the deep and dark step-off of the deadly drowning hole. They deserve your pity and your prayers because they are in the middle of the deadly drowning hole without the help of the divine Lifeguard. In the deadly swimming hole, swimming skills are useless, but everybody needs a lifeguard who knows how to rescue. God's people are summed up in the passage, "He suffered no man to do them wrong: yea, he reproved kings for their sakes; Saying, Touch not mine anointed, and do my prophets no harm" (Ps. 105:14-15, KJV). Abraham in Egypt, Isaac before Abimelech, Jacob in Padanaram, David in the wilderness, Daniel in the lion's den, and the Hebrew youths in the fiery furnace were vulnerable, but they were always under the blanket, of unconditional protection and divine providence.

B. Slippery Places

Truly God is good to Israel, even to such as are of a clean heart. But as for me, my feet were almost gone; my steps had well nigh slipped. For I was envious at the foolish, when I saw the prosperity of the wicked. For there are no bands in their death: but their strength is firm. They are not in trouble as other men; neither are they plagued like other men. Therefore pride compasseth them about as a chain; violence covereth them as a garment. Their eyes stand out with fatness: they have more than heart could wish. They are corrupt, and speak wickedly concerning oppression: they speak loftily. They set their mouth against the heavens, and their tongue walketh through the earth. Therefore his people return hither: and waters of a full cup are wrung out to them. And they say, How doth God know? and is there knowledge in the most High? Behold, these are the ungodly, who prosper in the world; they increase in riches. Verily I have cleansed my heart in vain, and washed my hands in innocency. For all the day long have I been plagued, and chastened every morning. If I say, I will speak thus; behold, I should offend against the generation of thy children. When I thought to know this, it was too painful for me; Until I went into the sanctuary of God; then understood I their end. Surely thou didst set them in slippery places: thou castedst them down into destruction (Ps. 73:1-18, KJV).

For both prophet and priest are profane; yea, in my house have I found their wickedness, saith the LORD. Wherefore their way shall be unto them as slippery ways in the darkness: they shall be driven on, and fall therein: for I will bring evil upon them, even the year of their visitation, saith the LORD (Jer. 23:11-12, KJV).

Let them be confounded and put to shame that seek after my soul: let them be turned back and brought to confusion that devise my hurt. Let them be as chaff before the wind: and let the angel of the LORD chase them. Let their way be dark and slippery: and let the angel of the LORD persecute them. For without cause have they hid for me their net in a pit, which without cause they have digged for my soul. Let destruction come upon him at unawares; and let his net that he hath hid catch himself: into that very destruction let him fall. And my soul shall be joyful in the LORD: it shall rejoice in his salvation (Ps. 35:4-9, KJV).

Slippery places are unsafe places, regardless of one's position. Slippery places always carry uncertain, untrustworthy, and unreliable futures. To be cast in dark and slippery places is to be haunted by the certain threat of double jeopardy. When one is slipping, his or her situation is growing worse. When a candidate is slipping in the polls, election chances are worsening. When the poll-slipping candidate is in the dark as to the reasons for the decline, recovery is elusive. When a patient's health is slipping and the physician is in the dark, the patient can become a victim of misdiagnosis. When a baseball batter's batting average is slipping and he is in the dark, his recovery could be unattainable. When your enemies are appointed by God to do duty in dark and slippery places, they become a greater threat to themselves than they could ever be to you.

Asaph was a spiritually gifted man. His impact upon Hebrew life has endured for centuries, yet he says in Psalm 73, "But as for me, my feet were almost gone; my steps had well nigh slipped" (v. 2, KJV). He was troubled as he beheld wicked men enjoying lavish lifestyles. He almost became a victim of the treacherous slopes occupied by those who judge according to what they see rather than what they know about the will of God. Asaph saw dishonest merchants cheat those who were unable to defend themselves. He saw cold-hearted men and women leave trails of tragedies, including the broken families that they had hurt without experiencing any consequences for their wicked deeds. He saw them enjoying the intoxication of ruthless power without any regard for man or God, and he wondered if serving the Lord was really fruitful. Then, something good happened to him. He said, "I went into the sanctuary of God; then understood I their end" (Ps. 73:17, KJV). In the sacred precincts of the house of God, he found the answer. Peace stole into his soul. A holy calmness lifted his head, and he saw things correctly. He caught a glimpse of the God who settles all accounts, and Asaph said, "Surely thou didst set them in slippery places: thou castedst them down into destruction" (v. 18, KJV). David also arrived at this conclusion in the thirty-seventh chapter of Psalms as he said,

> I have seen the wicked in great power, and spreading himself like a green bay tree. Yet he passed away, and, lo, he was not: yea, I sought him, but he could not be found (Ps. 37:35-36, KJV).

Herod Agrippa I Was on a Slippery Slope.

> Now about that time Herod the king stretched forth his hands to vex certain of the church. And he killed James the brother of John with the sword. And because he saw it pleased the Jews, he proceeded further to take Peter also. (Then were the days of unleavened bread.) And when he had apprehended him, he put him in prison, and delivered him to four quaternions of soldiers to keep him; intending after Easter to bring him forth to the people. Peter therefore was kept in prison: but prayer was made without ceasing of the church unto God for him. And when Herod would have brought him forth, the same night Peter was sleeping between two soldiers, bound with two chains: and the keepers before the door kept the prison. And,

behold, the angel of the LORD came upon him, and a light shined in the prison: and he smote Peter on the side, and raised him up, saying, Arise up quickly. And his chains fell off from his hands. And the angel said unto him, Gird thyself, and bind on thy sandals. And so he did. And he saith unto him, Cast thy garment about thee, and follow me. And he went out, and followed him; and wist not that it was true which was done by the angel; but thought he saw a vision. When they were past the first and the second ward, they came unto the iron gate that leadeth unto the city; which opened to them of his own accord: and they went out, and passed on through one street; and forthwith the angel departed from him. And when Peter was come to himself, he said, Now I know of a surety, that the LORD hath sent his angel, and hath delivered me out of the hand of Herod, and from all the expectation of the people of the Jews....And Herod was highly displeased with them of Tyre and Sidon: but they came with one accord to him, and, having made Blastus the king's chamberlain their friend, desired peace; because their country was nourished by the king's country. And upon a set day Herod, arrayed in royal apparel, sat upon his throne, and made an oration unto them. And the people gave a shout, saying, It is the voice of a god, and not of a man. And immediately the angel of the Lord smote him, because he gave not God the glory: and he was eaten of worms, and gave up the ghost. But the word of God grew and multiplied (Acts 12:1-11, 20-24, KJV).

Herod Agrippa I was an evil man descended from an evil line. This Herod was the grandson of one called Herod the Great. Herod the Great was the wicked king who commanded the slaughter of the children when he learned of the birth of Jesus Christ, thus fulfilling the prophecy that said "In Rama was there a voice heard, lamentation, and weeping, and great mourning, Rachel weeping for her children, and would not be comforted, because they are not (Matt. 2:18, KJV).

If you find it difficult to believe that Herod could order this slaughter, you should take note of his history outside what is recorded in the Bible. Someone described Herod as a "murderous old man." William Barclay wrote, "If Herod

125

suspected anyone as a rival to his power, that person was promptly eliminated." He murdered his wife Marianne and her mother Alexandra. His eldest son, Antipater, and two other sons, Alexander and Aristobulus, were all assassinated by him. Augustus, the Roman emperor, had said bitterly that it was safer to be Herod's pig than to be Herod's son. Something of Herod's savage, bitter, warped nature can be seen from the provisions he made near the time of his death. When he was 70, he retired to Jericho, the loveliest of all his cities, and gave orders that a collection of the most distinguished citizens of Jerusalem be arrested on trumped-up charges and imprisoned. By his order, the moment he died they would all be killed. He said grimly that he was well aware that no one would mourn his death, and he was determined that some tears would be shed on the day he died.

Herod Agrippa I was the brother of the wicked Queen Herodias, who instructed her dancing daughter, Salome, to have John the Baptist beheaded. Herodias hated John the Baptist because he spoke against her unlawful marriage to her brother-in-law. Upon the death of King Herod's father, Aristobulus IV, Herod's mother sent him to Rome in order to remove him from his grandfather's murderous hands. While in Rome, Herod Agrippa learned how to gain the favor of the royal family, particularly Gaius, the grand-nephew of Tiberius. When Gaius became emperor, Caligula gave Agrippa the title of king. Caligula later added Galilee and Perea to Agrippa's tetrarchies in southern Syria. Because his grandmother Marianne was a Hasmoneon princess, Agrippa used his Hasmoneon ancestry to gain the favor of his Jewish subjects. As he looked for ways to further win the favor of the Jewish leaders, he began to persecute Christians. To Agrippa, Christians were safe targets to attack. He had Rome's support. They had Rome against them. He had armies to support him. They had no armies and did not seek any. He didn't have religious endorsement for his efforts, but the Jewish authorities didn't seem troubled its absence.

The Bible sums up Herod's focus, saying, "He killed James the brother of John with the sword. And because he saw it pleased the Jews, he proceeded further to take Peter also." Herod could not see the Protector of God's people; therefore, he erroneously assumed that they had none.

Herod thought that people who were taught to turn the other cheek, love their enemies, and pray for those who persecuted them were safe targets to attack. He thought that those who worked to be peacemakers were not a threat because he made judgments according to the things that could be seen. He was blind to the secret source of the believer's strength. He expected no retaliation against his frenzied deeds. He was wrong, and so are your enemies when they fail to anticipate the factors that are unseen as they attack you. You can outlast and overcome them because of unseen realities that never fade. The apostle Paul put it this way:

> For which cause we faint not; but though our outward man perish, yet the inward man is renewed day by day. For our light affliction, which is but for a moment, worketh for us a far more exceeding and eternal weight of glory; While we look not at the things which are seen, but at the things which are not seen: for the things which are seen are temporal; but the things which are not seen are eternal (2 Cor. 4:16-18, KJV).

Herod had the apostle Peter arrested. He kept him in a maximum security ward. Peter was guarded by 16 soldiers, two chains, keepers, an iron gate, and two strong walls. Herod intended to bring Peter before the people after Easter and have him beheaded as he had done to James. God's ways are not our ways. God allowed James to die, but He chose to save Peter. God allows one child to be physically disabled, and He makes another child athletically gifted. Sometimes, God allows some to live for a long time, even while they are engaged in one wicked deed after another, yet He takes away a young person who seems to be bent on doing right and is blooming with goodness and righteousness. Sometimes, God seems to take angels and leave devils. Sometimes, good people hit hard times, and evil folk hit the lottery. But, regardless of how confusing life appears, there is something in the government of God that will make things right at the end.

I recall a story about a minister who visited an area known for the beauty of the throw rugs that were created there. As the minister moved about a rug factory, he was totally unimpressed. A tour guide noticed his displeasure and asked if he could help. The minister confessed his thorough disappointment at the products he beheld. The guide smiled and said, "Sir, I understand your problem. You are in the wrong line. The line you're in only shows the bottom part of the rugs. You're looking at the wrong side of the rug. This line is for those who want to see how strong the rugs are due to the interlocking of the threads that hold the rugs together." The minister changed lines, and when he saw the other side of the rugs, he was spellbound by their beauty. In this life, we can't see what God sees, and more often than not, we are looking at life from the wrong side. We do not see what the Master sees. If we will grow in grace and wait patiently on Him, one day, God will allow us to see the beauty of His work from the other side. How right was the poet who said,

> Be not weary for labor will cease, turmoil will change into infinite peace, wearisome burdens will all be laid down, then shall our cross be exchanged for a crown.

Herod discovered that Christians were not safe targets to attack. They are covered by the blood of Jesus. Easter let loose a new kind of power in the world. After Easter, Herod intended to destroy Peter, but the "God of peace, that brought again from the dead our Lord Jesus" did so "through the blood of the everlasting covenant" (Heb. 13:20, KJV). The blood of Jesus refers not only to the death of our Lord but also to His life after death. The blood of Jesus gives us a new life because the "life of the flesh is in the blood" (Lev. 17:11, KJV). On the night before Peter's proposed execution, he went to sleep. When you know that you are covered by the life-giving, life-protecting, and death-defeating blood of Jesus, you can go to sleep and leave your enemies in God's hands. The order to slay Peter had been signed. The date had been set. Peter was scheduled by Herod to die the next day. He ate his dinner, commended himself to the Lord, and went to sleep. Easter created a new life for a new Peter. The Church began to pray. God sent an angel. The angel touched Peter. His chains fell off. The door opened. The bolts slid. The lock turned. The iron gate swung open by itself, and Peter walked out, set free by the covenant of the new life won by the blood of Jesus.

After his defeat in Jerusalem, Herod did not repent. He left Jerusalem. The people of Tyre and Sidon had somehow displeased him. They bribed Blastus, the king's chamberlain, and he told them how to woo Herod with flattery. Josephus, the great Jewish historian, informs us that, on a set day, Herod stood before the people of Tyre and Sidon. He was dressed in a dazzling suit of silver. As he stood before the people with the sun shining upon the silver threads of his magnificent garment, he spoke. The people, in efforts to placate his anger, cried out, "It is the voice of a god, and not of a man." Herod had gone too far. The angel of the Lord smote him, and worms began to eat away at his viscera. For five days, Herod suffered on his sickbed, wracked by severe abdominal pains. The physicians couldn't help, and on the fifth day after the angel of the Lord smote him, Herod died. How slippery the platform was upon which he stood to make orations. How slippery the place was from which he heard, "It is the voice of a god and not of a man." How slippery the deed was for which God judged him. How slippery the spot was from which he slid from his sickbed, where the death dew sealed his fate. How deceiving appearances can be. In one moment, Herod stood as an oriental monarch who seemed invincible, and in the next moment, he was lying prostrate and crouched in the dust while worms were eating away the internal organs of his abdomen.

Vladimir Lenin, like Herod Agrippa, was a man who held great power and used that power for evil purposes. Lenin was the man who served as the mastermind behind the Communist Revolution in Russia. He unleashed his poison upon the world and had no reservations about liquidating any person who stood in his way. Lenin died on January 21, 1924. He had just finished trying some Catholic priests in Moscow. He had the archbishop and other priests marched through the streets as objects of hatred and derision. The very next night after his evil deeds, death came for him. First, Death stood by Lenin's bed and tarried for a while. From that hour, Lenin became a living corpse. Later, the autopsy performed on him revealed severe brain damage. The man who had thought so thoroughly about the implications of Communism suffered severe brain damage. It has been reported that he spent his last days crawling on all fours like a beast. How slippery the platform was from which Lenin fell before the almighty God, who marched his guilty soul into eternity to await the judgment that is to come.

How amazing verse 24 of the twelfth chapter of Acts is, which says, "But the word of God grew and multiplied" (KJV). Herod killed James, but the blood of a martyr became the seed of the Church, and "the word of God grew and multiplied." Joseph Lenin died an insane man, but the National Opinion Research Center at the University of Chicago released a study done during the 1990s that revealed a large percentage of conversions from atheism to faith in God. Andrew Greely, a sociologist at the University of Chicago, wrote an inspiring report on the findings and titled it "God Is Alive and Well and Living in Moscow." Greeley wrote, "It would seem, at least at first glance, to demonstrate that after the most serious attempts to obliterate religion in human history, they are experiencing the most dramatic religious revival in human history." According to the poll, 22 percent of the population in the former Soviet Union said they were once atheists but now believed in God. Tyrants come and go, but the Word of God continues to grow and multiply.

Child of God, you can, like Peter, "go to sleep" on the night before the day of your proposed destruction because you have a new life that no force can take. God's Word is true, His motives are pure, His rest is satisfying, His yoke is easy, His mercy is great, His blessings are many, His ears are attentive, His spirit is quickening, and His hands are outstretched.

> Recompense to no man evil for evil. Provide things honest in the sight of all men. If it be possible, as much as lieth in you, live peaceably with all men. Dearly beloved, avenge not yourselves, but rather give place unto wrath: for it is written, Vengeance is mine; I will repay, saith the LORD. Therefore if thine enemy hunger, feed him; if he thirst, give him drink: for in so doing thou shalt heap coals of fire on his head. Be not overcome of evil, but overcome evil with good (Rom. 12:17-21, KJV).

You don't have to toss and turn during the night, nor do you have to fret during the day. Our God is mighty. You can lay your head upon His bosom. He will raise you up, and He will see you through. Your enemies will be met by a force far greater than your own. Trust in God, for He is able to reveal the depth and power of your true self in ways far greater than you can comprehend. When God says, "Vengeance is mine; I will repay," He is telling you that you cannot bring about His purposes, but He can throw up a highway, and He can make the crooked paths straight.

It was during a time of great apprehension that Moses spoke prophetically concerning the tribe of Zebulun, saying, "For they shall suck of the abundance of the seas, and of treasures hid in the sand" (Deut. 33:19, KJV). Moses pointed to a time when Israel would become one of the greatest oil-producing states in the world. Today, oil-producing greatness belongs to the Arabs, but the day is coming when Israel will "suck of the abundance of the seas, and of treasures hid in the sand." Today, the treasures "hid in the sand" belong to the Arabs, but the promise made by Moses to Zebulun will be fulfilled, just as God's promise to you that He "will repay" is a fact that is waiting to happen. The end of God's work can never be doubted. Wrongdoing and wickedness may appear to be victorious on certain occasions, but the ultimate triumph of righteousness is assured. God is supreme; His Word is infallible, and His power is unlimited. Whatever God plans must come to pass. All you have to do is dwell "under the shadow of the Almighty" (Ps. 91:1, KJV).

CHAPTER IX

Your Enemies Don't Know that They Can't Rely on Their Past Successes to Determine Their Fate When They Go Against You

So Rab-shakeh returned, and found the king of Assyria warring against Libnah: for he had heard that he was departed from Lachish. And when he heard say of Tirhakah king of Ethiopia, Behold, he is come out to fight against thee: he sent messengers again unto Hezekiah, saying, Thus shall ye speak to Hezekiah king of Judah, saying, Let not thy God in whom thou trustest deceive thee, saying, Jerusalem shall not be delivered into the hand of the king of Assyria. Behold, thou has heard what the kings of Assyria have done to all lands, by destroying them utterly: and shalt thou be delivered? Have the gods of the nations delivered them which my fathers have destroyed; as Gozan, and Haran, and Rezeph, and the children of Eden which were in Thelasar? Where is the king of Hamath, and the king of Arpad, and the king of the city of Sepharvaim, of Hena, and Ivah? And Hezekiah received the letter of the hand of the messengers, and read it: and Hezekiah went up into the house of the LORD, and spread it before the LORD. And Hezekiah prayed before the LORD, and said, O Lord God of Israel, which dwellest between the cherubims, thou art the God, even thou alone, of all the kingdoms of the earth; thou hast made heaven and earth. LORD, bow down thine ear, and hear: open, LORD, thine eyes, and see: and hear the words of Sennacherib, which hath sent him to reproach the living God. Of a truth, LORD, the kings of Assyria have destroyed the nations and their lands, And have cast their gods into the fire: for they were no gods, but the work of men's hands, wood and stone: therefore they have destroyed them. Now therefore, O Lord our God, I beseech thee, save thou us out of his hand, that all the king-doms of the earth may know that thou art the Lord God, even thou only (2 Kings 19:8-19, KJV).

A. Undefeated Does Not Mean that You Can't Be Defeated

In this life, we are given only a piece of a jigsaw puzzle. It is always a mistake to act as if we've seen the whole puzzle and know exactly how and where all the pieces will fit together. When God is brought into the equation, everything changes. A lad's lunch is only two fish and five barley loaves; an invalid's fate is constrained by his 38-year history in the clutches of his misery; a woman's back is bent for 18 years; and a bully's threats seem to be a valid cause for sleepless nights until God is brought into circumstances. When God comes into the picture, all the "maybes" and "mights" are annihilated. They come to nothing. When God comes into the picture, what was trembles at the mercy of what He wants and what He wills. When God comes into the picture, the limitations of the past are broken, and good becomes available everywhere.

The position of God's people appeared to be hopeless, horrible, and shameful. Those who wore the garments of warriors trembled with agitation, hesitation, and timid apprehension. The arrogant heathen captain, Rab-shakeh, stood outside Jerusalem's wall with his battle armor gleaming in the sunlight. His fierce countenance reflected his determination. This man seemed to represent an enemy too strong to be resisted. City after city, kingdom after kingdom, and army after army had fallen before his ceaseless aggression, and the legend of his invincibility had spread throughout the land. The detailed movement of the heathen horde had been reported to Hezekiah, and vain had been the hope that the tide of evil would recede. The rumbling laughter of the enemy echoed around the wall. The mockery and banter of the Assyrian aggressor were revealed as he asked, "Hath any of the gods of the nations delivered at all his land out of the hand of the king of Assyria? Where are the gods of Hamath, and of Arpad? where are the gods of Sepharvaim, Hena, and

Ivah? have they delivered Samaria out of mine hand? Who are they among all the gods of the countries that have delivered their country out of mine hand, that the Lord should deliver Jerusalem out of mine hand?" (2 Kings 18:33-35)

Silence reigned among the people of God. A short period passed, and a letter was sent. Hezekiah didn't panic. He spread out the letter in the Temple before the Lord. What the enemy had said about his previous victories was true, but Hezekiah knew that a miracle is never too much to ask of the God of all miracles. May you take this moment to grasp this truth and gain the comfort you need in the face of every and any battle that you face.

1. **The God of All Natural Laws Can Suspend Any Law, at Any Time, Anywhere for His Purposes.**

Share your problems with God. Tell Him about them. You are never, ever alone or forsaken. Just as the God who lives above the mercy seat looked down upon the uplifted face of Hezekiah and read with invisible eyes the challenge of the Assyrian letter, so will He take notice of your issue. It doesn't matter if it's a pink slip, eviction notice, lawsuit, x-ray, or arrest warrant. Our God is a mighty Man of war. Share your problem with God. He knows what to do, and He is able to get it done. God essentially said to Hezekiah, "I've got this."

> And this shall be a sign unto thee, Ye shall eat this year such things as grow of themselves, and in the second year that which springeth of the same; and in the third year sow ye, and reap, and plant vineyards, and eat the fruits thereof (2 Kings 19:29, KJV).

God suspended the law of sowing and reaping and said that His people would reap what they hadn't sown. "Ye shall eat this year such things as grow of themselves."

2. **God Said, "I've Got This."**

> Because thy rage against me and thy tumult is come up into mine ears, therefore I will put my hook in thy nose, and my

135

bridle in thy lips, and I will turn thee back by the way by which thou camest...Therefore thus saith the LORD concerning the king of Assyria, He shall not come into this city, nor shoot an arrow there, nor come before it with shield, nor cast a bank against it. By the way that he came, by the same shall he return, and shall not come into this city, saith the LORD. For I will defend this city, to save it, for mine own sake, and for my servant David's sake. And it came to pass that night, that the angel of the LORD went out, and smote in the camp of the Assyrians an hundred fourscore and five thousand: and when they arose early in the morning, behold, they were all dead corpses. So Sennacherib king of Assyria departed, and went and returned, and dwelt at Nineveh. And it came to pass, as he was worshipping in the house of Nisroch his god, that Adrammelech and Sharezer his sons smote him with the sword: and they escaped into the land of Armenia. And Esar-haddon his son reigned in his stead (2 Kings 19:28, 32-37, KJV).

The Assyrians were cruel captors. They often tortured their captives for their own debased entertainment by blinding them and flaying the skin from their bodies until they died. If they determined that a captive was worth converting into a slave, they often would put a hook in the person's nose. God determined that He would treat the Assyrians in the same manner in which they had treated others. God spoke further, through the prophet Isaiah, explaining that the enemy would not besiege the city and that He would not even allow them to shoot one arrow into the city. How remarkable and awesome our God is. The enemy had 185 thousand soldiers who surrounded the walls of Jerusalem; of the 185 thousand soldiers, God did not allow even one of them to shoot one arrow into the Holy City.

God promised to defend the city for David's sake. How blessed we are that the Father will do even greater things for us for Jesus' sake. For Jesus' sake, God moves, and we can rejoice in saying,

Bless the LORD, O my soul; and all that is within me, bless his holy name. Bless the LORD, O my soul, and forget not all his benefits: Who forgiveth all thine iniquities; who healeth all thy diseases; Who redeemeth thy life from destruction; who crowneth thee with lovingkindness and tender mercies; Who satisfieth thy mouth with good things; so that thy youth is renewed like the eagle's. The LORD executeth righteousness and judgment for all that are oppressed (Ps. 103:1-6, KJV).

Dr. H. Clay Trumbull, a great man of God of a generation ago, related a story involving his young daughter. "She brought to me," he said, "a geography book, having on its cover a picture of the fabled Atlas, bearing the globe of the world on his shoulders." The small girl pointed to the over-burdened man, with his bowed head, tense shoulders, and distended muscles, staggering under the weight that seemed ready to crush him, and said, "Papa, why don't that man lay that heavy thing down?" Dr. Trumbull replied, "My dear, it would be better for him if he did. But that man has the idea that he must carry the world on his shoulders. There are a good many people like him, as you will find when you are older." Hezekiah didn't try to carry the world on his shoulders, and neither should you. God speaks to us during every unbearable moment, saying, "I've got this." If you will lay the heavy stuff down, you will discover the wisdom of the man who wrote, "Cast thy burden upon the Lord, and he shall sustain thee" (Ps. 55:22, KJV).

Faith in God will accomplish more work, establish more homes, satisfy more hearts, relieve more burdens, fulfill more hopes, and produce more joy than all other sources combined. Let no demon deceive you, regardless of its roar or its woe. All God needed to crush the Assyrian army, 185 thousand strong, was one angel. There are some who suggest that the "angel of the Lord" mentioned was some kind of suffocating wind that destroyed the Assyrian army during the night without noise, confusion, or warning. I find nothing to support that train of thought. I believe that the agent responsible for the destruction of the Assyrian army was a celestial being, as in the case of the death of the firstborn in Egypt (Exod. 12:29). If God is able to accomplish so much through one angel, consider what He is able to do with a legion of angels (Matt. 26:53).

Regarding their attacks upon you, your enemies may be undefeated. Like King Sennacherib, they might boast of their past feats and impressive victories. However, like Sennacherib, they have never faced the matchless power that is waiting to unleash itself as you call upon He who is only a prayer away. Wickedness, however triumphant, must end in ruin; and goodness, however threatened, shall end in glorious deliverance. The Bible informs us that Sennacherib's own "sons smote him with the sword."

The Bible often mentions the deaths of many rulers in a most cursory way. Only one incident is mentioned in the life of Herod the Great. Nothing is told of the Roman Emperor Augustus except his office and name; and not even so much as that is said of Augustus' successor, Tiberius. Yet, the Bible takes special care here to document the death of King Sennacherib, as it did Herod's, who was eaten by worms. After the king had returned to his own kingdom, the weapon he had so often used was employed on him by his own flesh and blood. The God who sometimes waits to be gracious often delays to destroy, but His patience should never be confused with His permission.

B. Being Told One Thing But Hearing Another

Long before King Hezekiah heard the voice of the prophet Isaiah, he heard the voice of the Holy Spirit speaking in his soul. The Assyrians told him to give up. They told him to consider their record, remember the defeat of their foes, and submit to their superior forces. They told him to accept defeat and to lay hold of their mercy. But, what they told him was not all that he heard. The great Dr. Gardner Taylor of Brooklyn, New York, helped me to discover this gripping truth as he delineated the struggles of the forebears of African Americans. For 246 years, with the complicity of government, hundreds of millions of Black people endured unimaginable cruelties. They were kidnapped, sold like livestock, and drowned by the millions during the terror-saturated voyages called the Middle Passage. They were subjected to backbreaking toil, beatings, rapes, castigations, maimings, imprisonments, and murders. They were told, often by so-called religious leaders who themselves were slaveholders, that God had ordained this sentence upon them. They were told that they were descendants of Ham—Noah's son—cursed by God to be slaves and servants of servants. They were told that they were born to be slaves. They would live only as slaves, and they would die as slaves. They were told that they were too weak, ignorant, powerless, and divided to be anything but slaves. That's what they were told, but they heard something else. They heard, "Before I'll be a slave, I'll be buried in my grave and then go home to my Lord and be free." They heard, "Great day! Great day, the righteous marching. Great day, God's going to build up Zion's Wall." They were told that creation teaches natural segregation—black birds don't fly with blue birds. But, regardless of what they were told, they heard, "Go down Moses—way down in Egypt's land. Tell Pharaoh to let my people go." They were told, "Find your place at the back. Get in your place at the bottom and stay there." But they heard, "Walk together, children. Walk together. There's a great camp meeting in the Promised Land."

The Assyrians told Hezekiah one thing, but the Spirit of God enabled him to hear another. He heard a voice that said, "Take your burden to the Lord and leave it there." He heard a voice saying, "The Lord is good, a strong hold in the day of trouble; and he knoweth them that trust in him" (Nah. 1:7, KJV). He heard a voice saying, "Though I walk in the midst of trouble, thou wilt revive me: thou shalt stretch forth thine hand against the wrath of mine enemies, and thy right hand shall save me" (Ps. 138:7, KJV).

"But they that wait upon the Lord shall renew their strength; they shall mount up with wings as eagles; they shall run, and not be weary; and they shall walk, and not faint" (Isa. 40:31, KJV). He heard a voice saying, When thou passest through the waters, I will be with thee: and through the rivers, they shall not overflow thee: when thou walkest through the fire, thou shalt not be burned; neither shall the flame kindle upon thee (Isa. 43:2, KJV).

Regardless of what you're told, it's up to you to decide what you will hear. This theme is further illustrated beautifully in the Book of Ruth. Naomi told Ruth to go back to Moab. Ruth, however, heard another voice speaking in her soul, and she said to Naomi, "Where you go I will go, and where you stay I will stay" (Ruth 1:16, NIV). Naomi said, "Go back" (v. 15, NIV). The Spirit of the Lord gave birth to another voice in Ruth's soul that said, "Come on. There is room in the city, and there is room in the Kingdom."

Ruth had undergone the sorrow of being made a widow while she was still young. God had a plan for her, and He has a plan for you. Submit yourself not to the voice of flesh and blood but to the voice of God's Holy Spirit. Don't allow the threats and barbs of the world to deafen you to the sweet voice of the Spirit of the Almighty within your own soul. Let your enemies speak. Don't argue—just refuse to hear them when they make your spiritual hearing dull and dim. If you submit yourself to the voice of God, you are yielding to an Architect who thinks in terms of the finished edifice and knows that you will stand in perfect peace one day in His presence. Michelangelo, as he hewed away at his block, would watch the chips fly under the heavy strokes of his mallet and chisel and would say to the interested student who looked on, "As the marble wastes, the image grows." Sometimes, through the attacks of enemies, some things that need to go are cut away from our lives so that the hidden beauty within us can be made visible to the world around us. Give God time. "He spends a summer on a rose that plays a simple role; an age upon each stream that flows forever on a soul." To be afraid of the attacks of enemies and painful things is to forfeit the peace that can be yours, even in the days when the chiseling is being done. Sometimes, a mean-spirited enemy is nothing more than a tool in God's engraving hand; that mean-spirited enemy could be the very tool by which He chisels out the finest features of the image of Jesus in your soul.

Don't struggle against God. Struggling against God never lightens a burden, nor does it lessen a sorrow. Let the threats come. Don't grow bitter. Don't complain. Don't broadcast. Don't dwell upon it, and don't force it upon others. Don't cherish it, and don't become so consumed by it that you shut your heart to heaven's comfort. Never forget that there is a gigantic difference between consolation and comfort; one comes from around you, and the other comes from above. The world might console you, but only God can comfort you. Never submit to the enemy, but always submit to the Father. If you rebel against God, that rebellion may halt the ministering angels who stand above, longing to help you. When you submit to God, you will gain the victory that comes when you lay your sorrowful condition at the Father's feet and accept what He sends. God knows what is best for you to endure in order to become your best. One day, it will all be made plain. If you allow Him, He will send billows of peace to sweep over your soul as you trust and walk by faith rather than by sight.

1. There is purpose in pain

Nobody loves pain, but the cessation of pain is not the greatest blessing you can hope for when experiencing physical suffering. The absence of pain does not necessarily equal the absence of danger. The presence of pain is often an indication of disease. As a matter of fact, pain is a blessing in the sense that it gives us a clue regarding an ailment. When correctly interpreted, pain paves the pathway for recovery and victory over disease. Your enemies don't know it, but the pain they bring into your life can increase your usefulness while God trains you for greater service. The record of humankind would be colorless indeed and without inspiration were it not adorned with the stories of those souls who have suffered their way into greater service. How many of us have been instructed, comforted, and strengthened because Bunyan had his sunless days of solitude in the Bedford jail, where he wrote *The Pilgrim's Progress*. It has been eloquently said that no one rightly suffers anywhere without contributing to the alleviation of human grief and to the triumph of good over evil, love over hate, and light over darkness. None of us live unto ourselves, and, therefore, none of us will die unto ourselves. In ways you can't see and I can't say, God, through your sorrows, sweetens the lot and strengthens the life of another who suffers near and after you. How right the soul was who said, "How sublime a thing it is to suffer and be strong."

2. God Is a God of Details

There is a purpose in all of the forces that touch and shape you. God is a God of unity. You will find a clear, scriptural illustration of God's unity if you look at the word *sweat* in the Bible. The word *sweat* only occurs three times in the Bible, and in each instance, there is a unifying thread. In the Book of Genesis, 3:19, God informed Adam, "In the sweat of thy face shalt thou eat bread," (KJV). In the Book of Ezekiel, 44:18, God says of the attire of the priests who served in the sanctuary, "They shall have linen bonnets upon their heads, and shall have linen breeches upon their loins; they shall not gird themselves with any thing that causeth sweat" (KJV). In the Gospel of Luke, 22:44, God speaks of the work of the Lord Jesus Christ in the Garden of Gethsemane prior to Good Friday: "And being in an agony he prayed more earnestly: and his sweat was as it were great drops of blood falling down to the ground" (KJV). Moses wrote that sweat was a direct result of Adam's sin of disobedience. Ezekiel reveals that a thousand years after Moses, priests were forbidden to wear any garment that would cause them to sweat when they shouldered the responsibility of their office as they ministered in the sanctuary. The priests were instructed to avoid garments that might cause them to sweat because sweat was identified with the curse of sin. It was about five hundred years later that Luke described the Lord Jesus Christ as being bathed in sweat like "great drops of blood falling down to the ground." Jesus, who bore the curse of sin, had to sweat because God "made him to be sin for us" (2 Cor. 5:21, KJV). Over a period of about 15 hundred years, God defines sweat as a curse; He uses the forbidden sweat of priests as a symbol of human helplessness; and He reveals that humankind had to wait for the Christ, who would completely heal the curse as He made His way to the cross while covered in His own bloody sweat. The God who allowed three writers, during a period of 15 hundred years, to record how He works out His redeeming purposes is patient and powerful enough to take all of the deeds done to you and use them all for His glory and your good.

There is a story about a ship on the St. Lawrence River, which was covered in a dense fog. The fog was so heavy that the lights onboard could only penetrate the air a few inches from the side of the ship. The passengers huddled together in despair. They asked an officer to speak with the captain, whom they could not find, and ask him to stop the ship and anchor down. The officer replied, "Don't worry. The fog we see does not extend too far above our heads. The captain you can't find is at the masthead, above the fog line. The captain can see clearly, and it is he who is directing the ship." Even in the darkest hour, God is directing both us and the events that touch us. We have no idea what will hit us in tomorrow's headlines, but we can be sure that God's sunshine will light us by day, and His unchanging star will burn for our guidance in the night.

There are some people who attend church and take for granted the grace of God. They make themselves enemies of God and good, and because they have not been cut down or cut off, they presume that they will not be. They are relying upon past deliverances from judgment or some foolish notion that they are immune to divine correction. They are wrong, and they are tempting God. When Satan urged our Lord to cast Himself down from the pinnacle of the Temple because God's angels would hold Him up, Jesus said, "Thou shalt not tempt the Lord thy God" (Matt. 4:7, KJV). When your enemies attack you and feel that they can continue to do so with no heavenly intervention, they are tempting God. They don't know that their repeated aggression places the Holy Spirit in a position where His wisdom and power are at war with His mercy and grace. Most people do not see their aggression and deception clearly. They often develop pretty euphemisms, clever rationalizations, and light-hearted ways to diminish the seriousness of their sin in God's sight and its consequences for them. Attacking God's child is a serious and dangerous business. God is jealous over His Church and His children.

When Ananias and Sapphira lied to the Holy Spirit in the fifth chapter of Acts, the Holy Spirit acted in judgment. A death sentence was passed upon them and no time was given for repentance. The Church is not only a happy place, but also a holy place. If people in a church are after you, please pray mightily for them. They are treading on dangerous and deadly ground. They are tempting God. The seriousness of an act is always in proportion to the office of the person against whom the sin is committed. It is a serious matter to tempt an earthly judge; it is a matter beyond words to tempt God. When the Holy Spirit struck down Ananias and Sapphira in judgment, He did something that Jesus had never done. There is not one recorded instance in which Jesus struck down any person in judgment. This act of judgment is one of those biblical examples in which God makes clear what He thinks of a matter. God struck down Sodom and Gomorrah for their evil and smote kings Uzzah, Uzziah, and Sennacherib in order to reveal fully how He feels about certain matters. Those who simply want the fringe benefits of the Christian faith while working to harm Christians would better serve themselves by keeping their distance from the Church. The Bible sums up the results of the Holy Spirit's intervention:

> And great fear came upon all the church, and upon as many as heard these things. And by the hands of the apostles were many signs and wonders wrought among the people; (and they were all with one accord in Solomon's porch. And of the rest durst no man join himself to them: but the people magnified them) (Acts 5:11-13, KJV).

3. Discipline Results from Training, and Punishment Comes as a Penalty

God, in His wisdom, might allow the deeds of an enemy to discipline you, but He will never give unlimited power to your enemy to punish you. A criminal is punished for the crime he has committed; a child is disciplined to salvage the good he might do in the future. God sees, God knows, and God determines when we need a lesson.

The story is told of a Christian blacksmith. He was a man who had known many sorrowful tests. A skeptic confronted him and asked him to account for the fact that he had sorrows in spite of his faith. He replied, "I don't have all the answers. I don't know if it is possible for a man such as myself to account for the things that have happened to me to your satisfaction, but I can account for them to my own joy. Sometimes, I take a piece of iron and bring it to white heat and then strike it to see if it will take temper. Then, I plunge it into water to change the temperature suddenly and then again into the fire. Finally, I put it on the anvil, and with the hammer, I make it into a useful article. If it will not take temper and respond to blows, I cast it on a pile of scraps. I have tried to bear the afflictions of my Father as patiently as I could, and every day, I say to Him, 'Lord, put me in the fire, if You will; put me in the water if You see I need it; do anything You think best, but Father, please, for Christ's sake, don't throw me on the pile of scraps.'" If God takes away pain, He must also take away the power of the soul to endure the strain. If God takes away the pity that knits hearts to hearts, He must also take away from us the capacity to give. If God releases us from loving one who is difficult to love, He also denies us the character and integrity birthed out of our sacrifice. If, in His wisdom, God allows the wrath of an enemy to discipline you, it will prepare you to do good in the future.

CHAPTER X

Your Enemies Don't Know that You Are Invincible Until You Complete God's Will for Your Life

And all they in the synagogue, when they heard these things, were filled with wrath, And rose up, and thrust him out of the city, and led him unto the brow of the hill whereon their city was built, that they might cast him down headlong. But he passing through the midst of them went his way (Luke 4:28-30, KJV).

The synagogue crew had Jesus within their sights, not within their prerogative. God let them rise up and lead our Lord unto "the brow of the hill," but He passed through them unhurt...no...that is not precisely what the Bible says. It says, He passed "through the midst of them and went His way." Jesus didn't outrun them or fly above them; He miraculously passed "through the midst of them." His time was not up. His hour had not come. God, the Father, ordered His steps, just as He orders yours, and He limited the power of His enemies, just as He limits the power of your enemies. In the Garden of Gethsemane, our Lord suffered as He prayed. In the court of the priests, "Some began to spit on him, and to cover his face, and to buffet him, and to say unto him, Prophesy: and the servants did strike him with the palms of their hands" (Mark 14:65, KJV). In Pilate's hall, they abused our Lord, but they could not kill Him until He had completed God's will for His life. The Roman soldiers scourged Him, but they could not stop Him. The cross was not the idea of man, but the will of God.

A. We Have an Appointment; No Man Can Rush or Postpone It

There is an apocryphal story that tells of a merchant and his servant in Baghdad. In the marketplace one morning, the servant saw a troubling figure pointing at him. Knowing it to be the death angel, he ran home and begged a horse of his master so that he could flee to Dothan before nightfall. His master agreed to give him the horse, and the servant rode off as quickly as possible. Later that day, the merchant was walking through the marketplace and saw the death angel. Being an extremely bold man, he walked up and asked, "Why did you make that threatening gesture at my servant this morning?" The death angel replied, "It was not a threatening gesture but a gesture of surprise. I didn't expect to see him in Baghdad. You see, I have an appointment in Dothan with him tonight."

No matter how far or fast we run in the opposite direction, we all have an "appointment in Dothan." It is a God-given appointment. When God is ready, He will dismiss us from these mortal bodies of ours, and we will pass through the gate of death into a more glorious life. We have no need to fear any figure, system, or person. If we are faithful to our noble calling, we will impact the world far more than the world will impact us. The examples of men who desired to impact the world are countless. Publius Cornelius Scipio was the Roman general who invaded Africa and defeated Hannibal of Carthage, but it was at a tremendous cost of Roman lives. Scipio's hatred was so intense that, before his death, he made arrangements for his sepulchre to be placed so that his image might stand facing toward Africa. It was Scipio's hope that, even while dead, he might still be a terror to the land that produced a warrior king of the magnitude of Hannibal. At his death, his strange orders were followed, but he did not create any sense of terror either for the youngest child or for the most frail among the sick of Carthage.

Prior to his death, Cardwallo, the ancient king of Great Britain, commanded that his dead body be embalmed and bronzed and then placed on a bronze horse over Ludgate, in order to be a terror to the Saxons. But, when Cardwallo died, the Saxons rejoiced instead of trembled at the sight of his bronzed body. When Zisca, the magnificent Bohemian, neared his death, he charged the Tabonites to flay his corpse and make a drum from his skin. It was his hope that, when the drum made from his skin was beaten, the enemies on the battlefield would be put to flight and his soldiers would become lionhearted. But there is no record that his death inspired legions or defeated masses.

How different is the outcome of our Lord's death and the deaths of all who faithfully serve Him. Some make the mistake of holding the envy of the Pharisees, the treason of Judas, the desertion of the Eleven, Pilate's injustice, Herod's actions, and the cruelty of the Roman soldiers responsible for our Lord's death. The truth is, the outward agents of Calvary were but instruments to bring God's great purpose—humankind's redemption—to pass. God the Father not only numbered the days of Jesus, He also, in His matchless wisdom, appointed the means to convey Him out of the world. It was Charles Drelincourt who said centuries ago, "Therefore, when we see the strangest accidents come to pass, and the most unexpected tragic deaths before our eyes, we must remember the saying of the prophet Jeremiah when he saw the burning and plunder of Jerusalem: 'Who is he that saith, and it cometh to pass, when the Lord commandeth it not?'" (Lam. 3:37, KJV).

God alone is able to make our lamp go out, and He is able to use an external force to blow the light out. The great source of comfort that belongs to Christians is that our God can and will light our lamps again by the undying beam of the Son of righteousness and will so light us that we will shine forever, gloriously, in the highest heavens.

Daniel could not die in the lions' den, and Joseph could not die in the pit or in the prison because God's will had not been completed for either life. There is a promise which says, "And it shall come to pass in the day that the Lord shall give thee rest from thy sorrow" (Isa. 14:3, KJV). "Grief," said Benjamin Disraeli, "is the agony of an instant—the indulgence of grief is the blunder of a life."

A small boy was riding a bus. He gave his seat to an elderly lady who was weary from her day's work. The lady objected at first by saying, "Son, I hate to take your seat, but I am really tired," as she sank into the proffered seat. The boy replied, "That's all right. I only have a little ways to go." Your degree of faithfulness depends not upon the amount of endowment. You can be faithful with a few things or many things; the dedication is equally great whether you are given a lot or a little. You must never permit your enemies to so trouble you that you fear what they might do to you. Emerson once said, "He only is rich who owns the day; and no one owns the day who allows it to be invaded with worry, fret, and anxiety."

B. God Is Faithful in All Things

The God who tracks the journey of 100 billion stars in each of 100 million galaxies knows the path, the history, and the future of every speck of dust in His cosmic space. He calls each of us to preach His entire Gospel with balance and clarity. "For God hath not given us the spirit of fear; but of power, and of love, and of a sound mind" (2 Tim. 1:7, KJV). When we approach every foe and every fact with the belief system that our God is faithful, He empowers us to become living witnesses of the truth of His testimony and the favor of His faithfulness.

In a great cathedral during the Middle Ages, there was a magnificent stained glass window. Travelers from all parts of the world braved the trek to look upon the splendor of that great work of art. One day, ominous clouds gave birth to a

massive storm that shattered the window into small fragments. The local worshipers were grieved by the ruin of their
proudest external possession. They gathered the pieces and
packed them away. Later, a stranger arrived and was
informed that the window, which he had traveled miles to
see, had been shattered. He asked for the broken bits, which
were readily given to him because they appeared to be of no
further use. Time passed, and one day an invitation arrived
for those who attended the cathedral. The invitation was
from an artist known for his unique skills in glass-craft. He
asked the people to come to his place of work to evaluate a
work of brilliance. Upon their arrival, the artist drew aside
the veil that covered his work, and as the people looked, they
saw the most beautiful mosaic they had ever seen. As they
stood there marveling at the beauty, the artist replied, "This
window that I have made came from the fragments of your
shattered one, and now, it is ready to be replaced." The
Cathedral thus possessed, instead of a stained glass window,
a marvelous mosaic.

Even if your life plans are shattered, God is faithful. He is
able to make blessings more exquisite than you have ever
dreamed emerge from catastrophes. God is faithful. He has
promised to hear you when you pray, supply when you are
in need, give when you ask, open when you knock, reward
when you seek, and satisfy when you desire. He has promised to warm your heart, build your faith, open your eyes,
calm your nerves, dry your tears, and feed your soul. He has
promised to be the Confidant that assures, the Prince that
redeems, the Abundance that supplies, the Wealth that
enriches, the Staff that supports, and the Provision that
satisfies.

C. God Transforms Leanness into Abundance

God loves to take His people from the lean lowlands of
lack to the high holy hills of abundance. Those who are
unable to look back to days that afforded genuine satisfaction

can face the brighter prospect of the pull of the future. "And Joshua said unto the people, Sanctify yourselves: for tomorrow the Lord will do wonders among you" (Josh. 3:5, KJV). If you cannot see the mighty hand of the Almighty in your yesterdays, lift up your head and cast your searching eyes upon Him in your beckoning tomorrows.

How I love the story about the man who had nothing for his family to eat. He went hunting with an old gun and two bullets. He saw a rabbit, aimed, shot, and missed. Down to his last bullet, he heard a voice say, "Pray first, aim high, and keep focused." He looked up and saw a turkey in a tree, but then he heard a noise, looked down, and saw a rattlesnake coiled between his legs. The voice spoke again, saying, "Pray first, aim high, and stay focused." He obeyed. He prayed, took aim, and shot the turkey above his head out of the tree. The bullet went through the turkey, killed it, and lodged in the head of a twelve-point buck deer. At the same time, the handle of the gun fell and killed the rattlesnake between his legs. The kick from the discharge thrust him backward, and he fell into a pond. When the man came up from under the waters, he had a turkey and a deer to take home. The snake was dead and he had fish in all of his pockets. He had obeyed the heavenly mandate to "pray first, aim high, and stay focused," and he quickly made the journey from the state of "not enough" to the place of "more than enough."

If you will believe God's Word, trust God's promises, respect God's power, defer to God's wisdom, and be grateful for God's provisions, you will prevail in places where others panic and are brought down. The apostle Paul says, "Being confident of this very thing, that he which hath begun a good work in you will perform it until the day of Jesus Christ" (Phil. 1:6, KJV). God finishes what He starts. He began a work in you at your hour of salvation, and no force can halt His work prior to its completion. Nobody can short-circuit God, draw a line that He cannot cross, or erect a barrier that He cannot annihilate. God has no Waterloo. God cannot fall or fail. Even when people point out your failures, they cannot call an end to your race.

Our sins and our sorrows can be wiped out by the obliterating grace of God. The poet Louise Tarkington once spoke of the hope of honest souls, "I wish that there were some wonderful place/called the Land of Beginning Again/Where all our mistakes and all our heartaches/And all of our poor selfish grief/Could be dropped like a shabby old coat at the door/And never put on again."

Our darkest thoughts, deepest hatreds, and most vexing worries can be consumed at the altar of God's mercy and grace. Our mistakes, misstatements, and heartaches can be dropped like a shabby old coat and never put on again. The summons from Isaiah instructs us, "Come ye, and let us go up to the mountain of the Lord...and he will teach us of his ways, and we will walk in his paths" (Isa. 2:3, KJV).

In the Steven Spielberg movie *Saving Private Ryan*, a squad of soldiers is sent on a mission to rescue one soldier from behind enemy lines. Their orders are simple. They are to find Private Ryan and bring him home. It is a costly undertaking. Most of the men in the squadron, including the commanding officer, are killed in their noble quest. As he lies upon foreign soil and speaks his last words, the commander addresses Private Ryan. He says, "Earn this." He reminds the private that good people have died to save him. Strong men have painted the battlefield crimson with their blood. "Earn this" is a charge given to one whose freedom has been purchased at a supreme cost by those who have paid the supreme price.

As an elderly man, Sgt. Frederick Niland, on whose story *Saving Private Ryan* is based, visited the grave of his courageous benefactor. As he knelt at the grave, he said, "Not a day goes by I don't think about what happened, and I just want you to know, I've tried. I tried to live my life the best I could, and I hope that's enough. I didn't invent anything. I didn't cure any diseases. I worked a farm. I raised a family. I lived the best I could, and I hope, in your eyes at least, I earned what you did for me."

Though the forms and forces of evil are countless and malignant, God is with us. The perfect gift of Jesus Christ, our Lord, has set us free to live, love, and long for Him. He is able to save us from what seems to be inevitable wreckage. He calms those who look to Him and face up to their duty. The Holy Spirit whispers, if you will hear, His reminder of Calvary, "Earn this." As we progress in this journey, we are obliged "to leave the old with a burst of song, to recall the right and forgive the wrong" (Rbt. Brewster Beattie). God is able to give you the wisdom and the strength to drop your heartaches like a shabby old coat and never put them on again. In addition to the strength to drop yesterday's "old coats," there is a buoyant confidence that comes to those who have a mission here and a destination elsewhere. The devil is busy, but we must resist him. We are not ignorant of his devices. His attacks come from familiar sources. His methods have changed little since he tempted our first parents in the Garden of Eden. He spoke disparagingly of the Word of God. He charged God wrongfully and plunged into utter falsification. Today, he still casts doubt upon the Word of God through weak and sometimes wicked people. Satan also will use a discouraging set of circumstances to entice you to doubt both the Word of God and the God of the Word. Don't walk in the way of the flesh, but walk in the way of faith.

During the dark days of World War II, King George VI would sometimes speak to the British people over the radio. After a very difficult time, when the allied forces were in disarray, the king spoke to the nation. Much of what he said during that time has been forgotten, but the poem he quoted by Mary Louise Haskins has inspired generations: "And I said to the man who stood at the gate of the year: 'Give me a light, that I may tread safely into the unknown!' And he replied: 'Go out into the darkness and put your hand into the Hand of God. That shall be to you better than light and safer than a known way.' So, I went forth, and finding the Hand of God, trod gladly into the night. And He led me toward the hills and the breaking of day in the lone east." Those who walk in the faith find something "better than light" and something "safer than a known way." You can get it if you walk in the faith. Jesus had it; this is dramatically illustrated in our Lord's exchange with Pilate.

> Then saith Pilate unto him, Speakest thou not unto me? knowest thou not that I have power to crucify thee, and have power to release thee? Jesus answered, Thou couldest have no power at all against me, except it were given thee from above: therefore he that delivered me unto thee hath the greater sin (John 19:10-11, KJV).

If we will walk in the faith, patterning our lives according to God's Word, we can be victorious over satanic attacks, to the glory of God. Jesus forever lives to make intercession for all of His children (see Heb. 7:25). His petitions for us will be answered if we will only trust Him. God remains. There is an eye that never sleeps beneath the wings of the darkest of nights. There is an ear that is never deaf. There is an arm that never tires when the greatest human strength gives way.

On December 28, 1991, the anti-God Soviet Republic (USSR), brought into being by Lenin and Stalin, fell and rose no more. When the first Russian satellite reached outer space, some in Russia said, "Creation from a communist point of view is at last under new management." But only God proposes and disposes. The USSR fell. God remains while nations crash. The psalmist says in Psalm 102, "Of old hast thou laid the foundation of the earth: and the heavens are the work of thy hands. They shall perish, but thou shalt endure" (vv. 25-26, KJV). God remains. The Hebrew word for "remain" means "He sits undisturbed forever." God not only endures; He endures without being upset, confused, or sidetracked. God remains. There is nothing that can stop God or stop you before His will is complete for your life. There was nothing that could stop Him—or you—yesterday. There is nothing today, and there will be nothing tomorrow to stop you short because there is nothing that can stop God at all. There is a wonderful scene in John Bunyan's *The Pilgrim's Progress*. As the pilgrim, whose name was Christian, moved toward the city of his hope, he experienced some setbacks. But Christian continued his journey toward the bright city. On one occasion, he was thrown to the ground, but he struggled back to his feet and cried out to his opposition, "Don't rejoice yet, for every time I fall, I shall rise again." The apostle Paul, possessed of the same determination that drove Christian toward his shining city, declared,

> For God, who commanded the light to shine out of darkness, hath shined in our hearts, to give the light of the knowledge of the glory of God in the face of Jesus Christ. But we have this treasure in earthen vessels, that the excellency of the power may be of God, and not of us. We are troubled on every side, yet not distressed; we are perplexed, but not in despair; Persecuted, but not forsaken; cast down, but not destroyed (2 Cor. 4:6-9, KJV).

D. God Prepares His People for Eternity

There is a force in us that resists an existence that is limited by time. We search for ways to rise above the fact that our years, our hard-won gains, and our cherished achievements will eventually be snatched from our hands. With a parrying acceptance, we acknowledge time's unmerciful sickle that cuts a wide swath across our years and strikes down things that we define as precious. We search for ways to stand in proud defiance of the damage that time can do, and we admire those brave souls who tackle the effects of time with some success. It is Tennyson's Ulysses who, as an aged warrior, says,

> "Tho' much is taken, much abides; and tho' we are not now that strength which in old days moved earth and heaven; that which we are, we are; one equal-temper of heroic hearts, made weak

by time and fate, but strong in will to strive, to seek, to find, and not to yield."

What a magnificent soul is this Ulysses. He says, "Much is taken." He was old, tired, and spent. Yet he also says, "Much abides." We admire Ulysses, but we know that there are boundaries beyond which such an intrepid spirit cannot go because time, in the end, defeats the best of human courage. But, thanks be to God that we can, through faith in Christ, find an unshakable courage with which to defy time. Our faith speaks of eternity. Our hope is an eternal hope. Our home beyond this world is an eternal home. God has placed time into eternity. In the midst of the swift and swelling changes of time, there is that which is constant, abiding, and eternal. Human life is transitory, but God's goal for us is eternal. This earth shall perish, and like a vesture, one day it shall be folded, but the life that God desires for us shall never end. God's Word speaks forcefully and confidently of those things that last forever: "Thy throne, O God, is forever and ever" (Ps. 45:6, KJV). "The Lord shall reign for ever" (Ps. 146:10, KJV); "And I will pray the Father, and he shall give you another comforter, that he may abide with you for ever" (John 14:16, KJV); "Jesus Christ the same yesterday, and today, and for ever" (Heb. 13:8, KJV); "And they shall reign for ever and ever" (Rev. 22:5, KJV).

1. **The eternal God calls us to believe in that which is eternal.**

"The eternal God is thy refuge, and underneath are the everlasting arms" (Deut. 33:27, KJV). Our political parties come and go. Our tastes change. Our sizes change. "But thou art the same, and thy years shall not fail" (Heb. 1:12, KJV).

2. **The eternal God challenges us to establish a relationship that is eternal.**

In the eighth chapter of Romans, Paul runs the entire gamut of hurts, hazards, threats, and tragedies and concludes that nothing can "separate us from the love of God, which is in Christ Jesus our Lord" (8:39, KJV). Even the dearest and most precious human relationships are fragile and are subject to powerful forces bent on destroying them. The relationship established between the spirit and the Savior cannot be broken by anything in time or eternity on earth, in hell below, or in heaven above.

3. The eternal God crowns us with possessions that are eternal.

Jesus spent His life teaching people the difference between treasures on earth and treasures in heaven. Earthly treasures are perishable and can be easily snatched from our hands. The treasures of heaven are imperishable. They can be kept forever. Heavenly treasures are beyond the destructive power of moth, rust, thieves, financial ruin, and physical death (see Matt. 6:19).

4. The eternal God creates in us something that will be eternal.

Today, we are living in an eternal dimension. "And this is life eternal, that they might know thee the only true God, and Jesus Christ, whom thou has sent" (John 17:3, KJV). Our present bodies are not equipped for eternal life, but God will give us bodies in His own time equipped for eternal ages.

Be of good cheer. God will see you safely through the opposition.

> And when there arose a great dissension, the chief captain, fearing lest Paul should have been pulled in pieces of them, commanded the soldiers to go down, and to take him by force from among them, and to bring him into the castle. And the night following the Lord stood by him, and said, Be of Good cheer, Paul: for as thou hast testified of me in Jerusalem, so must thou bear witness also at Rome (Acts 23:10-11, KJV).

Paul's enemies did not and could not have their way. God had work for Paul to do in Rome. Satan is always behind the efforts of enemies who seek to derail us short of our God-given destinations, but God is personally committed to see us safely beyond the false finishing lines erected by men. Whenever you are under fire for your faith, expect divine intervention. It seems evident that, when Satan caused our first parents to sin, he wrested from them the authority with which God had intended them to rule over His dominions. From that dark hour to this day, Satan has been the prince of this world. Both the physical world and humankind have been under his evil control. This is clearly revealed and illustrated in the temptation of the Lord Jesus Christ (Matt. 4:8-9, KJV). Satan showed Jesus a panoramic view of the kingdoms of this world. He offered to give to Christ those kingdoms if He would fall down and worship him as God. Some scholars make the mistake of minimizing the satanic offer, but the proposition was bona fide. It was bona fide because Satan had ruthlessly seized control of this earth from Adam. Jesus came into the world to regain from Satan the authority that he wrongfully possessed.

God's only method for dealing with Satan was to deal effectively and completely with the matter of sin. Sin gives power to Satan. When sin entered the Garden, Adam and Eve became slaves to it. Satan, who had brought about their fall, assumed his limited control. While God holds ultimate control of this world, He refrained from instantly destroying Satan in order to bring about a final and comprehensive reckoning with sin. Your enemies get their power from Satan, and Satan gets his power from sin. Jesus Christ came into this world to deal with sin once and for all. Jesus Christ is, in Himself, God's total answer to sin. Whereas the penalty of sin was death, the death of Christ, the sinless Lamb, fully paid the penalty. But, praises be to God, death and hell are overcome. The price has been paid. Punishment for the sinner is anulled by the death of the sinless Substitute. The major reason I can tell you, with confidence, that God will see you through the opposition of your enemies is because He has already seen us through by destroying the penalty of sin.

> For when we were yet without strength, in due time Christ died for the ungodly. For scarcely for a righteous man will one die: yet peradventure for a good man some would even dare to die. But God commendeth his love toward us, in that, while we were yet sinners, Christ died for us (Rom. 5:6-8, KJV).

How can I tell you that the Lord will destroy and nullify the deeds of your enemies that are meant to stop you short of your goal? I can do so because He already has destroyed and nullified the authority of Satan. It was through the cross that Jesus bore at Calvary that the false claims of Satan were invalidated. It was through the cross, in all its naked horror, that God secured the victory for Himself and His children. Through the work of the cross, deliverance and freedom for all those enslaved by Satan have been won. Satan's defeat, which had been prophesied (Gen. 3:15), was accomplished. "And having spoiled principalities and powers, he made a show of them openly, triumphing over them in [the cross]" (Col. 2:15, KJV). Jesus Christ knows tomorrow far better than we know yesterday. In Him, we see the perfect Person. In Him, we see the "fulness of the Godhead bodily" (Col. 2:9, KJV). In Him, we see God's perfect standard laid out for all the ages.

It is said that the wives of the fishermen along the Adriatic Sea had a custom of going to the seashore at night and singing a stanza of a familiar hymn. They would then listen until they heard, borne by the winds, another stanza of the same hymn, sung in answer to theirs by their husbands. To the heart that listens in the dark, there will always come songs of comfort and cheer, across the night and the storm.

E. God Stands by His People

Your enemies don't know how determined God is to save you from resentment. Not only are you invincible until God's will is complete for your life, but you also have the power to recover from resentment. The cross of Jesus Christ enables you to let go of the hurt. If you hold on to hurt, it becomes resentment, and if you hold on to resentment, it becomes hatred.

Regardless of what others have done to you, God can make the rest of your life the best of your life.

God raised Jesus up from the dead to make sure that you would know that He will stand by you in both life and death. He will stand by you when friends are few and enemies are numerous. They put Jesus in a tomb at the foot of a hill. They sealed the stone in order to seal the tomb. They made it secure. In a sense, their efforts succeeded; they shut God out of their hearts. The seal held, but not for long. Easter morning arrived, and the earth was unable to hold the King of kings. God added an exclamation point to the story of humanity's history. Jesus broke the seal and came out of the grave.

Sometimes, people can hurt you by ignoring you. They can hurt you by failing to acknowledge that you exist. Don't be resentful. God has already acknowledged you when He broke the seal on the tomb of Jesus. God had an earthquake ready to liberate the saints who had died, and He already has one ready to liberate you, regardless of whether you've been sealed out or sealed in. God's Word is true, His love is real, His name is holy, His ways are just, His yoke is easy, His mercy is great, His promises are sure, His spirit is quickening, His hands are outstretched, His peace is perfect, His works are righteous, and His burden is light. Our God fortifies us against failures. He guarantees success when we venture out in faith. The prophets and apostles and many of the saints of God have gone on ahead of us, but the same God has led the way, and it is He who will stand by us to see us safely through.

PRAYERS

1. Over Cruel Words

Lord, awaken my memory to Your Word, and help me to revisit and review Your mercies. I know from Your Word that pride and deception are subtle enemies. I bless You, at this hour, for sending my Savior, Your Son, Jesus Christ, to travel the roads of this life. I ask You, Father, to equip me with the determination to pay no heed to cruel words and stinging rebukes. Help me to lay hold of the truth that many men will not speak well of Your servants. I understand that there is a time for acquiring and accomplishing and that there also is a time for resting and refueling. Teach me how to discern the difference, and always keep me grateful for the time to both work and rest.

True authority is a gift from You, and it is beyond the influence of demons, kings, traditions, and political figures. How I praise Thee that no person has power against me except it be given to them from You. No words are uttered by enemies except those You permit, and if You permit the words, You will make them work together for good. In the name of Christ, I pray. Amen.

2. For the Forgiveness of Sin and the Bottling of Tears

Father God, who speaks through creative words and exceptional deeds, I bless You for the ways You comfort me during my hours of contention. I thank Thee that I know and understand the pain that sin creates. I no longer see my sins as minor infractions but as major impediments. In uncommon ways, You have taught me about the high price You have paid. I open my heart and repent of anything that separates me from You. Father, forgive me for the times I have been dazzled by material gifts. It is the assurance of Your love that has brought me this far and will keep me. The very thought that You have not only forgiven me of my sin but have bottled my tears leaves me in a state of perpetual gratitude for the freshness of Thy mercy. I stop at this moment so that my soul can sing of Your longsuffering grace that has followed me as I have traveled and has been patient with me as I have rebelled. Thou art great and kind, and I pray for a voice in every wilderness to tell of Your countless blessings. My enemies are right. You have been better to me than I deserve, and I love and praise Thee for every act of mercy that You have brought my way. In the name of Christ I pray. Amen.

3. Over Good Days in Bad Times (Ps. 91)

Our Father and our God, how we rejoice that You are able to give us good days even in the worst of times. Despite the evil intentions and open aggression of our enemies, You continue to do great things in feeble lives. Even in the worst of times, You satiate our thirst and feed our souls with bread that is not of this world. I now see how You glorify Your name as You protect Your own from the terrors of the night and from the dangers of the day. It is because of Your favor upon me and all that is mine that I dread no plagues that stalk in the darkness and no disaster that might strike at midday. You have told me in Your eternal Word that, though a thousand fall at my side and ten thousand fall around me, no evil will touch me. I believe Your promises. I take Thee at Thy word. I know that Your retribution may seem slow in coming, but in the end, it will overtake the fleet of foot and do Thy biding at the right time. I will not focus my eyes upon the prosperity of the wicked, but I will scan the horizon for acts of Your goodness, and I will enjoy blessings that no curse can nullify. I claim my blessings, regardless of the darkness of the times or the boast of the ungodly. I will not fret. I will not faint. I will not despair. I will see good days because nothing can separate me from Your love. In the name of Him who is the Alpha and Omega, I pray. Amen.

4. For Promotions that Come in Spite of Efforts to Harm

Father, I thank Thee that those things done to harm me have in the past and will in the future work out to promote me. You have put into me the need to be confident, and I will make no effort to escape that need. I surrender to Thy sovereignty. I bask in your habit of flipping the script. I live by a faith that is not imposed on me dogmatically but is written in me intrinsically. Father, I thank Thee that, while You do not need my worship, You desire it. You do not need my companionship, yet You invite me into Your unchanging presence. You do not need my service, and yet You enlist my help. With thanksgiving, I bow before You in prayer and commit my energies to learn and do Your holy will.

I know that Satan will oppose me, but I am not afraid. I understand that people will misunderstand and, at times, misuse me, but I am not afraid. I know that this world is no friend to grace, but I am not afraid. I bless You that You are Lord of all. At Your words, storms are stilled, armies are defeated, diseases are healed, and even the dead are raised. I will fear no efforts against me because I know that, by Your mercy, possibilities become fact and opposition can fan the flame of a burning light that will never fade. In the matchless name of Jesus, I pray. Amen.

5. For Making Evil Deeds Fall Out of Bounds

Dear Father, You alone are worthy to be worshiped. You have made self-serving and self-preserving works fall short of their intended goals. Neither the profiteering work of Judas nor Pilate's disregard of justice has sealed my doom. You have opened my mind to the soundness of Thy teachings. I rejoice in knowing what I know. I have been through both the deepness of the waters and the heat of the fire, and You have refused to let evil works defeat my soul and darken my sanity. Foolish men have sought to ignore Your Word, even as others have sought to undermine Your will, and yet their works have not afforded them victories. In some instances, You permitted men to kick us, but they ended up kicking us upstairs. You, who raised up Jesus Christ and made Him Lord, have shown both Your heart and Your hand in countless tender mercies and promotions. In the name of Jesus Christ, I pray. Amen.

6. Over Those Who End Up in Our Debt

Father God, Thy kingdom is an everlasting kingdom, and Thy dominion endures throughout all generations. You have revealed Your desire to go with us through every circumstance. You have shown me that You can change people and positions. I know that the first can be made last and the last can be made first. Daily, You awaken us to the journey of life, and You try us in many ways. I pray for the grace to be merciful to those who have hurt me and are now under my authority and power. Teach me how to be forgiving and how to live without harboring any hostility. Let me not become absorbed with my own pain. Gentleness and kindness are of Your Kingdom. Help me not simply to seek Your blessings but also Your authority. Show me how to love those who have hated me. Teach me how to forgive those who need my forgiveness, regardless of whether or not they ask for it. Disturb, by Your Word, my complacency, and forgive, by Your grace, my lethargy. I know that I can do all things through Christ which strengtheneth me (Phil. 4:13, KJV). I now know that I can rise to my full powers if I shed my hurt and march forth to meet life with a triumphant faith. Let it be so, I pray. In the name of He who Thou hast raised from the dead, I pray. Amen.

7. Over Those Who Don't Know Who They Are Not

Eternal God, I thank You that my enemies are not experts on my abilities. I praise You that my life is in Your hands. When temptations call me, I sometimes forget that You are the One in whom we live, and move, and have our being (Acts 17:28). Help me to say to my soul when enemies forecast my demise that the joy of the Lord is my strength (Neh. 8:10). Speak to me wherever I might be, and give me a responsive heart to answer the urgings of Your Holy Spirit. Enable me to focus upon You as my life's source and meaning. Help me to add value to Your community of faith. Move us to be of one accord, devoted to the redeeming work made visible in the sacrificial death of our Lord and Savior, Jesus Christ. Lord God, I pray for the wisdom to know that my greatest asset is that which gives priority to Thy purposes and Thy plans. How I praise Thee that, in spite of evil and evildoers, there is an island of sanity amid the roaring and raging seas of confusion and conflict. Help me to be a worthy part of Your glorious fellowship of those whose hearts have been touched and whose lives have been redeemed. In His holy name, I pray. Amen.

8. Over Enemies Who Have Dates to Do Duty in Dark and Slippery Places

Heavenly Father, I cannot praise Thee enough for Your greatness. You control all nations. You determine the outcome of every war. You repay both good and evil according to a wisdom that is above earth-born minds. I thank Thee for the holy occupations of intercession and supplication. I willingly and joyfully offer myself to Your schedule. I will not give You a deadline because I know that You are an on-time God. I bless You, Father, for eyes to see and a heart to perceive Your justice, which overtakes the enemies of goodness and righteousness. I have seen enemies vocal and strong in days past and gone, but today, their names are forgotten and their voices are no longer heard. Surely, You have placed those who harm Your children in dark and slippery places. You have allowed us to overcome the devil by the blood of the Lamb and by the Word of our testimony (Rev. 12:11). I rejoice that You are able to both conquer and confound every enemy. As with David's sling and five smooth stones, You have, by simple things in the hands of Your servants, created miracle after miracle. I now proclaim Your majesty. I have learned great lessons in the dark that I could not absorb in the brilliance of a rising sun. In the name of He who is the perfect Lamb of God, I pray. Amen.

9. Over God's Power to Overrule History

Father God, in a world where many worship technological, political, financial, literary, corporate, and analytical power, I rejoice in worshiping You, the God of all power. I thank Thee that Your holy power stands in stark contrast with the power of man, who is here today and gone tomorrow. Thou art a God whose power is not only consistent with Your Person but also consistent with Your patience. You have allowed sinners to sin and boasters to boast and given to each time to repent. You have knocked at the doors of the hearts of men by giving them victories when they should have been victims. You have walked through the deep places of life with a guiding light and a helping hand. In strong and silent ways, You have led and invited us to follow. You have protected me, and I gladly define myself as a partaker of Your grace and a recipient of Your comforting words and gentle care. I pray for the strength to meet Your challenge that calls for an uncompromising commitment. I have seen You move through promotions and demotions; I have heard You speak through the voice of both victory and defeat. Renew now, O God, my memories of Your grace so that, as I recall the past, I will also hear You calling me into the future. In the name of Jesus, I pray. Amen.

10. For Making Me Invincible Until My Work Is Finished

Heavenly Father, You have rescued me when I could not escape the clutches of doom, defeat, and death. You have given me eyes to see that Your law is birthed of Your love and that Your justice is always tempered with Your grace. If my enemies could have, they would have totally destroyed me by now, but You did not let them. Your precepts are right, giving joy to the heart (Ps. 19:8). My eyes are averted because Your holiness is too great for human eyes to see, so I bow my head in humility and admiration. I thank Thee that I am not in the hands of men. I praise Thee for divine protection day in and day out. I rejoice in Your faithfulness. You hold me in Your hands. No man, system, demon, or devil can pluck me out of Your safety zone. Your law is perfect. It revives my soul, and I will rest serenely and securely in Your Son's finished work at Calvary. In our Lord's name, I pray. Amen.

Talahase Flordia
Billy Graham
Sat M. 12-27 -14
1-877-772-4559
WLJC
Call for Prayer
To ORDER
CALL

TAlKed ABOUT MOXN
MilKiNg 30 COWS NIGHT
/ B Graham evun Com.
DePT. DC C
Chas. NC 28201

Printed in the United States
90466LV00003B/1-174/A